"I read this excellent book with a mixture of gratitude and sadness: gratitude for the wisdom offered for leaders in the church and beyond who are charged with handling reports of sexual harassment and abuse, and sadness that I did not have this tool sooner. Bluhm weaves her own experiences with carefully researched information that sheds light where we most need to see and face the truth. I encourage you to read with an open mind and heart, ready and willing to play your part as an advocate for justice and healing. We can and must do better."

—**Nancy Beach**, leadership coach, Slingshot Group; author of *Gifted to Lead: The Art of Leading as a Woman in the Church*

"I've often believed that something is wrong when we have believers who are passionate for God yet who lack compassion for the wounded and interest in the truth. Tiffany's story is a compelling and necessary look into what happens when 'loyalty at all cost' is put before truth. Her words are a clarion call to believers to finally do the work of holding genuine space for the wounded and the abused, especially when that means having to be critical of ourselves and our institutions."

—**Leslie Nwoke**, founder, HeartWork Now

"As a survivor of abuse and exploitation, I have discovered the undeniable power of breaking the silence. In *Prey Tell*, Tiffany provides readers with two invaluable gifts: brilliantly excavated insight into the systems and practices that silence women, and a roadmap to finding our voices and helping others to find theirs. This timely and important work is sure to open eyes, shatter barriers, and unleash justice."

—**Harmony Grillo**, author of *Scars and Stilettos*; founder of Treasures

"*Prey Tell* sounds the alarm on both the obvious and more subtle forms of misogyny that are all too common—both inside and outside the church today. Every chapter is filled with silence-breakers sharing their stories of harassment and assault, and through their brave honesty, readers are invited to advocate for a better path forward. As a woman in church leadership for close to two decades, I believe this book is an absolute must-read!"

—**Nicole Smithee**, CEO and co-founder of Iridescent Women

"Bluhm brings passion, insightful research, and biblical conviction to the problem of the harassment, manipulation, and silencing of women. As one who has experienced this treatment while also finding healing and wholeness on the other side, Tiffany is uniquely positioned to help the reader understand not only why and how this abuse happens but also the practical actions each one of us can take to stop it. As a man who serves in leadership, this book will help me to serve as an advocate for the women around me."

—**Bobby Arkills**, executive director, Tacoma Area
Youth for Christ

"I devoured *Prey Tell* in one sitting. Every page is rich with compelling true stories, Scripture, and statistics that describe the experiences of women everywhere. Tiffany offers hope for the future, strength for the reader, and solutions for creating communities where women are helped and not harmed. Men and women in positions of leadership, as well as women recovering from abuses of power, will benefit from the wisdom and insight Tiffany provides. This book is timely and necessary."

—**Ashley Abercrombie**, author of *Rise of the Truth Teller*,
cohost of the *Why Tho* podcast

"For anyone wondering how abuse happens, and why a victim of abuse might not speak up for years, Bluhm does an exquisite job dissecting the factors of power that come into play—gender, discrimination, wealth, and seniority—and creates a map to understanding the dynamics that make abuse possible. She then provides steps to allyship in the fight toward building safe systems that dignify women. This is an important read for anyone who's been silenced or done the silencing: in short, everyone."

—**Blythe Hill**, CEO and founder, Dressember Foundation

"Bluhm offers clear, concise, and compelling insights on the whys and hows of the silencing of women, offering straightforward steps to end it. She quashes the all-too-common stereotypes and myths about abuse with well-documented and thorough research. If you want to grow in your love and advocacy for women, read this book. My copy is chock-full of highlights. I will return to it again and again."

—**Eric Schumacher**, coauthor of *Worthy: Celebrating the Value of Women*; cohost of the *Worthy* podcast with Elyse Fitzpatrick

PREY TELL

WHY WE SILENCE WOMEN WHO TELL THE TRUTH AND HOW EVERYONE CAN SPEAK UP

TIFFANY BLUHM

BrazosPress

a division of Baker Publishing Group
Grand Rapids, Michigan

© 2021 by Tiffany Bluhm

Published by Brazos Press
a division of Baker Publishing Group
PO Box 6287, Grand Rapids, MI 49516-6287
www.brazospress.com

Library of Congress Cataloging-in-Publication Data
Names: Bluhm, Tiffany, author.
Title: Prey tell : why we silence women who tell the truth and how everyone can
    speak up / Tiffany Bluhm.
Description: Grand Rapids, Michigan : Brazos Press, a division of Baker
    Publishing Group, [2021]
Identifiers: LCCN 2020038312 | ISBN 9781587434785 (paperback) | ISBN
    9781587435355 (casebound)
Subjects: LCSH: Civil rights—Religious aspects—Christianity. | Human rights—
    Religious aspects—Christianity. | Women's rights—Religious aspects—
    Christianity. | Sexual abuse victims. | Sex discrimination against women.
    | Women's rights. | Power (Christian theology) | Respect for persons. |
    Christianity and justice. | Women in Christianity.
Classification: LCC BT738.15 B59 2021 | DDC 250.82—dc23
LC record available at https://lccn.loc.gov/2020038312

The author is represented by Joy Eggerichs Reed on behalf of Punchline Agency,
LLC.

21   22   23   24   25   26   27   7   6   5   4   3   2   1

To those who lent me their strength in my darkest hour,
I am forever indebted to you for your kindness.

She sings beautiful and slow
A tune that only caged birds know.

—"MY LOVE GOES FREE,"
LYRICS BY JON FOREMAN

CONTENTS

Contents

Part 3: How Everyone Can Speak Up

ACKNOWLEDGMENTS

Joy, thank you for your belief in the role of the bystander. Your representation and encouragement in this process have proven invaluable. I adore you, your side buns, and your insight into life. You are more than my agent, you're a kindred spirit. Merci beaucoup!

Katelyn, I can't thank you enough for how you've steered this text in the right direction and brought the best out of me. As I've said before, working with you is winning the literary lottery.

To the Brazos team, thank you for your efforts in preparing this book for the men and women who will glean from its pages.

Ashley, your friendship and encouragement will forever be treasured. With your morning voice memos and late-night text messages applauding my efforts, you were the sideline cheerleader at the mile markers I needed to cross the finish line on a book that demanded so much of my heart and mind.

Jana, what a gift you are to me. You've inspired me to take my place and sing a redemption song. Thank you for your support as I speak up on behalf of our sisters everywhere.

Harmony, thank you for your vital feedback and wise perspective as I wrote this book. Your lifelong fight against the exploitation of women has inspired me to stand for women, even when it cost me more than I ever thought I could give.

Melisa, your passion and discernment have been a gift for the past twelve years. Even when I couldn't see how God could redeem or restore the story, you reminded me that he was working, working for the good of the vulnerable.

Gigi, your discernment and willingness to stand for the dignity of women will forever be remembered. Lending your strength to me when I was running on empty reminded me that this is not a fight we must ever attempt alone. We are stronger together.

Holly and Derek, thank you for your love, encouragement, long talks, meals shared, and baked goods to sustain me through the last year of outlining and writing this book. You are family to me and mine.

Jessica, thank you for your bold support throughout the last decade. You've always reminded me just how much the Shepherd cares for his lambs. May we always be fierce protectors of the vulnerable. And may our brows be on point.

Anchor Church, you've been the harbor for the broken and the base for the sent that you claim to be. In your community of imperfect people, what was lost and stolen from my family has been restored.

Derek, I'm eternally grateful for your commitment to me, my career, our children, and our God. Our life together has taken many turns, but I'm devoted to colaboring with you until the very end. You are my equal, my partner, and my lifelong love.

To my children, Jericho and Kingston, thank you for knocking before you barged into the office while I wrote this book. Once you are older, and you learn of its contents, may you be inspired to use your voice to stand with women—your sisters, daughters, and aunties.

And finally, to the silence breakers, your bravery and grace is a witness to the goodness of God. I am honored to walk alongside you, and although we may have passed through fire, we don't smell like smoke. Our God was with us all along.

INTRODUCTION

The practice of silencing women is not a female issue, male issue, Democrat issue, Republican issue, Black issue, white issue, Asian issue, Latinx issue, indigenous issue, evangelical issue, mainline issue, upper-class issue, middle-class issue, or lower-class issue. It's an everyone issue. It permeates every field, sector, and pocket of society. It happens to fast food employees, high-powered executives on Wall Street, educated and affluent medical doctors, Hollywood actresses, assistants making minimum wage, everyday churchgoers, and devout clergy. In short, it's happening everywhere. And unless we pursue the redemptive arc of justice, it will continue uncontested, and half the human population will suffer under the weight of abuse and violation.

At the time of this writing, hundreds of men in high-profile positions have been ousted in recent years, according to news reports. Their last names make us cringe. Weinstein. Nassar. Lauer. Ailes. O'Reilly. Epstein. Kelly. Savage. Crist. Hybels. Their actions were made known to the public by brave women who found the courage to tell their story, journalists committed to telling the truth, and whistleblowers who refused to stand idly by while a woman—and in many cases, several women—were disgraced.

Most of us learn of an abuser's nefarious actions on the nightly news or through articles shared on our newsfeeds. As we discover an abuser's dark and twisted antics, we reel at the thought of someone acting so unequivocally depraved. We ask ourselves the questions everyone is asking: How did he get away with it for so long? Why didn't anyone report him before now? Why were these women falling for his games? Why did they let him do that? Why didn't the board do anything sooner? Weren't there rules and accountability in place to prevent such things? And why, in this day and age, is the abuse of power at a woman's expense still par for the course?

As men are accused, and some even convicted in courts of law, many of us turn our questions to the women: What kind of woman would find herself in these situations in the first place? Does she have values? Where are her morals? What was she wearing? Did she ask for it? Was she leading him on? Did she blackmail him? Is she on a power trip? Is she making it up for attention? Why would she do this to him? Is she trying to ruin his marriage? Does she have a Jezebel spirit? Who does she think she is?

These questions imply that the onus is on the woman to avoid and escape abuse more than on the man to control his behavior in the first place. Somehow, as a society we have determined that *she*, not his own actions and choices, is responsible for his downfall.

Even with major political and cultural strides for women over the past one hundred years or so, the practice of silencing women after they've been entangled in emotional manipulation, sexual harassment, or assault has evolved to fit the form of modern life. It's taken on a complex shape that still, without fail, robs a woman of her voice to speak up and receive the care and healing she needs to move forward with her life.

There must be another way. In a #MeToo world, we can argue for greater transparency, accountability, and prevention. We can push for laws and procedures that protect women, and we can join others in boldly telling our stories of abuse at the hands of powerful predators. Sadly, at the very same time, we can be seen as opportunistic, unforgiving, unbiblical, spotlight seeking, and vindictive—with a vengeance for blood. Angry feminists out to win any semblance of power we possibly can as we crush the patriarchy and ruin a man's life and family, all for selfish gain. In reality, we are women—and men—who witness the silence and slander of women and cannot stand to see misconduct so poorly handled in this cultural moment.

As people of faith, we may be tempted to sit this one out and avoid engaging in this conversation, for fear we'll get it wrong, be misunderstood, be stereotyped, or stand alone, when what is needed in our families, workplaces, organizations, churches, and communities is the honest truth and action. When our world is shaken upside down by a man who abuses his power, it's human nature to react with fear—to shrink, hide, zip our lips, and move far, far away from the issue. We vow never to utter the truth to anyone, and we're convinced our plan will work, until it doesn't.

Stories of silencing women may not be anything new, but they continue to wreak havoc on the lives of women and weaken the movement toward equality. This book examines the outcomes when we silence, slander, and then, finally, believe women. It tells of what happens when we speak truth to power and spend ourselves on behalf of justice. It tells of losses, undeserved grief, and lessons learned about why we silence women and the emotional, financial, and societal ramifications of doing so. As you turn every page of this book, may you find your own way, your own voice, and your own conviction for standing with women and believing women when they've been wronged, and together may we bend the arc toward justice, where it belongs.

For the purposes of this book, when I describe someone abusing power, I have chosen to use male pronouns. While women can silence and slander other women (which I will address), and while women also abuse power, biblical and modern history suggest that the abuse of power for sexual exploitation has overwhelmingly been done by men, while women are overwhelmingly the ones being abused and silenced. As a warning to readers, this book contains descriptions of sexual harassment and violence that may be triggering to those who have been harmed by these behaviors.[1]

Following are some terms used in this book as defined by the Rape, Abuse, and Incest National Network (RAINN).

> *Sexual harassment* includes unwelcome sexual advances, requests for sexual favors, and other verbal or physical harassment of a sexual nature in the workplace or learning environment, according to the Equal Employment Opportunity Commission (EEOC). Sexual harassment does not always have to be specifically about sexual behavior or directed at a specific person. For example, negative comments about women as a group may be a form of sexual harassment.
>
> Although sexual harassment laws do not usually cover teasing or offhand comments, these behaviors can also be upsetting and have a negative emotional effect.
>
> Sexual harassment can occur in a variety of circumstances. The harasser can identify with any gender and have any relationship to the victim, including being a direct manager, indirect supervisor, coworker, teacher, peer, or colleague.
>
> Some forms of sexual harassment include:
>
> - Making conditions of employment or advancement dependent on sexual favors, either explicitly or implicitly.

- Physical acts of sexual assault.
- Requests for sexual favors.
- Verbal harassment of a sexual nature, including jokes referring to sexual acts or sexual orientation.
- Unwanted touching or physical contact.
- Unwelcome sexual advances.
- Discussing sexual relations/stories/fantasies at work, school, or in other inappropriate places.
- Feeling pressured to engage with someone sexually.
- Exposing oneself or performing sexual acts on oneself.
- Unwanted sexually explicit photos, emails, or text messages.

. . . *Sexual assault* refers to sexual contact or behavior, often physical, that occurs without the consent of the victim. Sexual harassment generally violates civil laws—you have a right to work or learn without being harassed—but in many cases is not a criminal act, while sexual assault usually refers to acts that are criminal. Some forms of sexual assault include:

- Penetration of the victim's body, also known as rape.
- Attempted rape.
- Forcing a victim to perform sexual acts, such as oral sex or penetration of the perpetrator's body.
- Fondling or unwanted sexual touching.

Sexual misconduct is a non-legal term used informally to describe a broad range of behaviors, which may or may not involve harassment.[2]

PART 1

WHY WE SILENCE WOMEN WHO TELL THE TRUTH

The problem has never been the ways that victims don't tell, so much as it has been that some victims aren't seen as valuable to protect.

—MIKKI KENDALL, *HOOD FEMINISM*

1

EVERYTHING IS JUST FINE

There he was, ten feet in front of me in broad daylight. There was no mistaking him for someone else. To my advantage, I spotted him from behind the tinted windows of my car, where he couldn't see me, yet I could watch him. Of course, I knew the day would come when our paths would cross, but I never guessed it would happen without him ever knowing.

Truth be told, up to that point I feared his presence so severely that I avoided his local haunts and had been successful in maintaining my distance. Yet there he was. With a pounding heart and shaking hands, I held my breath and clenched the steering wheel as he crossed the street in front of me. As he passed, one step in front of the other, the most remarkable thing happened—I survived. Time froze so I could be afforded a moment to realize that his hold over me was gone. Before he vanished from sight, I whispered, "I won't give you power over me. Not anymore."

I found it terribly odd that, the very same day I saw that man walking down the street when I sat crouched in my car, I had read a lengthy piece about a publicly beloved man's untoward actions behind closed doors. Women who had previously worked for the well-known icon disclosed stories that painted him in an unfavorable light in the country's most distinguished newspaper. Their stories reminded me that my own story was not to be despised but rather to be honored for how it had given me a deep commitment to justice, truth telling, and accountability. Yet for me, the penny was still in the air. That man on the street, by the looks of it, was going to get away with all he had done with zero ramifications or consequences. It seemed as though he had won—and I had lost more than I would have ever dreamed. He held the power; I did not.

You see, for the majority of my life I had made it my mission to keep men who held power in my life pleased with me, to stay on their good side, and to do as I was told. I played by their rules and hardly questioned their authority. Every boss I've ever had, except for one (thank you to the beautiful Korean woman who managed the Quiksilver outlet), has been a well-resourced white man. Every pastor I've ever had, including my grandfather, has been a white man. On top of that, in nearly every setting I grew up in, I was the only minority, the token brown girl in a sea of snow white. My nickname in high school, printed on the back of my cheer sweatshirt and catcalled through the halls, I kid you not, was "brown girl." As an agreeable, conflict-avoidant woman of color, rather than voice any concern when I spotted discrepancies or experienced othering, I mastered silencing my own voice in order to be of value to the world around me, especially to the men who employed or pastored me. This is what postcolonial theorist and Columbia University professor Gayatri Spivak describes when minorities, in an effort to have power, contort themselves to manifest it in a way that is recognizable and acceptable to those who ultimately hold it.[1] I could fit your definition of acceptable to ensure you felt comfortable with my presence.

As an adopted girl from East India raised in a rural white community with white parents and male siblings, I never thought to question the hierarchy, as I was conditioned to believe that the world was ordered for men of means to hold power and for people like me, those who didn't fit the order, to fall in line and take whatever scraps were given to us. This implicit belief was reinforced in textbooks, in movies, by the government, at hourly wage jobs, from the pulpit, and even on notoriously racist billboards along the highway. Women were second to men, and minority women sat at the end of the line. Men set the rules, defined their meaning, and enforced said rules. Growing up, I wish I'd known of the strides women had made worldwide to be recognized as equals, to be seen as dignified and worthy of respect—how women marched, lob-bied, and fought against patriarchal practices in the halls of power that demeaned, silenced, and slandered them. I wonder if I would have gleaned from their strength and stories, believing that another way was possible: one where women, even marginalized, minority women, have a place that is not inferior but necessary.

Even if I did learn of Toni Morrison, bell hooks, Savitribai Phule, the Grimké sisters, or Sojourner Truth, it was hard to believe that equality was possible when one of my earliest, most terrifying memories was playing in the yard of the neighbor girl's house when her dad, with a shotgun in tow, screamed at me to get off of his lawn and "go back to where you came from." I heard him loud and clear and ran as quickly as my little legs could carry me through their field, across the street, and up my driveway, straight into my house, where I hid in my room. I was seven. The very next day at school, my friend said nothing of the encounter between her dad and me. She never spoke of it, and neither did I. I, as a young brown girl, was inferior, and that white man, forty years my senior, with his shiny black gun, was superior. I would not be convinced otherwise.

After I graduated from high school, my understanding of a woman's place in the world expanded as my grip on justice tightened, but I still held to this conscious, and subconscious, belief that if I held even a shred of power, it was because someone with privilege (in my case, white male privilege) had given it me. Many of my pastors, bosses, teachers, and mentors, to their credit, were outrageously gracious, kind, and generous. To them I owe so much. They believed in women, married strong women, and gave me opportunities I would have never had otherwise; however, they still remained in charge of women. Many of them treated that power with the utmost respect; others abused it beyond what I could have ever imagined.

Like many other women, I've made excuses for the men in my world. *He didn't mean it like that. That wasn't his intent. He's a good guy. I'm sure he has my best interest at heart. He is the one God chose to lead me. He sees the whole picture. He knows change takes time. He means well, but boys will be boys.* I made excuses until I couldn't. Until my convictions outweighed my loyalty.

Faux Egalitarianism

From the first moment we meet him, we know he is different. We can't help instantly liking him as he comes in for a tight handshake, one hand in ours and the other nestling our elbow. A smile spans ear to ear. In a world where women are ushered to the back seat, ignored, or hired as a token of inclusivity, it's a surprise to meet someone who enthusiastically welcomes women as equals. His presence is refreshing, and his charm, palpable. Even better, we never went looking for a boss/coach/mentor/pastor like him. He found us. He tells us how humbled he is that we would entertain the opportunity of serving him.

As we get to know him, he asks questions about our personal story. He's caring and fascinated about how we have collected the life experience we have. He might ask about our family or if we are dating anyone. You know, normal get-to-know-you stuff, we tell ourselves. Even though he probes into our personal life, he makes us feel like he cares about knowing us beyond our skill sets, gifts, connections, and references. With everything he says, every question and comment, we feel more and more at ease. Free to be our honest self: not a woman attempting to fill a man's place in the world, but a woman with skills, passions, and knowledge to excel. He doesn't seem aloof or out of touch with how the world treats women in the workplace, in politics, in sports, in entertainment, in education, or in the church. He condemns those who do not treat women as equals, and he's the kind of man with power and privilege we dream of, one who will use it to advance the place of women—or so we think.

Right out of the gate, he makes it clear to those around him that we are capable, worthy of respect. A force for good and a welcomed asset in his life. He gives us opportunities that we are shocked to receive and take ever so seriously. If he ever receives pushback from others over our place in his orbit, he defends us. His commitment to a woman's place in the system is more than theory. He knows what we are capable of and pushes us to be the best version of ourselves. He makes time for conversations that always crescendo with encouragement of the woman we are becoming. He does everything in his power to advance our trajectory in the world. We are in a perpetual state of fangirl joy as his personal warmth relentlessly matches his public praise of us.

Perhaps another perk of serving, working, or partnering with him: he regularly asks for our opinion on what could be different. It isn't unusual for him to ask for feedback, and together we collaborate on improving the system we are in. There are only a handful who are privileged enough to be asked what they think, and we are honored to be among them.

Referring to the men in his world, he mentions that they don't get him like we do. They've been around forever and are set in their ways. He needs us to get where he wants to go, and we understand what it takes. He convinces us that we have a special connection with him that is unlike other connections with the men and women in his life. He tells us that together we can move the needle; we know how to do it, and we have what it takes.

Truthfully, we admit, he is everything we want to be. Relentlessly creative, sharp, successful, a visionary, and appearing to dignify the existence of everyone he meets. He doesn't present himself as untouchable but comes across as a man interested in the well-being of others. His approach becomes the gold standard for us. He seems to care for everyone he meets—he memorizes names, recalls complex details of someone's personal story, and checks in on a regular basis. He positions himself as not only a boss, coach, professor, or spiritual leader, but also a mentor and promoter. He introduces us to people with power as if we are their equal and praises our accomplishments in front of strangers. Anytime we are around him, we feel proud to be associated with him. Everyone's ways are antiquated, but not his. He understands the power of a smart woman, and by his own admittance, he lets her run free. He is the champion that every woman pursuing equality hopes for.

We hardly question his investment in us. We give him the benefit of the doubt and feel no inkling to question his motives. We, along with the others he's convinced of his persona, believe in him, his upright character, and his rapidly growing vision for us.

Even if some of his comments make us feel sick to our stomach. Like when he says,

- "We really need a female perspective to round things out here."
- "No one would listen to you if you weren't so beautiful."
- "You're my proud diversity hire."
- "Wow, you look stunning in that dress."
- "Girlie, you get it. I know you hear me."
- "Teach these old guys something new, sis."
- "I love the way you wear your hair like that."
- "Maybe we could talk about your promotion over lunch."
- "We need to see you on the stage more. Everyone likes it."
- "We don't want her leading the prayer meeting, they need eye candy. Ask someone skinnier."
- "Well, I think women have their place and voice, certainly, but we still know at the end of the day someone has to make the hard decisions and not everyone is going to agree."
- "No one ever complained about this before—are you sure this isn't just a personal issue or vendetta? Give us facts, not emotions."
- "We aren't trying to silence anyone, just appear as a united front."
- "Of course you're allowed to speak up, but, personally, I've never seen what you're mentioning happen."

He never makes these remarks in front of a crowd, mind you, only behind closed doors, where the one subject to his insensitive comments feels too indebted to him to speak up.

His comments pile up in the recesses of our mind. We sometimes ride the wave of his compliments just as others do. He makes us feel noticed and highly esteemed, even if, at times, it is for our looks, but of course we don't always feel esteemed. We feel degraded. If he makes a low blow, others might clap back with a snappy comment about how hard they have worked to be heard, how diligently they have labored to be taken seriously, but we don't respond this way. We don't want to lose our opportunities. We don't want to lose his favor. We don't want to lose everything we have worked so hard to build. We weigh the odds, and it doesn't seem worth it to question his comments. We receive it for what it is, because, like so many others, he is not only a mentor to us but also a promoter. We feel as though if we are going to advance in the world, it will be because of him. Faux egalitarianism at its finest.

Trapped in a Broken System

Women weigh the odds and count the costs of speaking out. They choose to remain silent in order to collect a paycheck, advance their careers, be accepted in their churches, engage in opportunities to lead, and, truthfully, stay in the place they've worked so hard to access. They know the drill: Look like a ten. Be the smartest person in the room, but don't act like it. Keep your fears and nervousness to yourself. Be insanely agreeable. Laugh on command. Be nice.

In my earliest days of working in a professional setting, I learned how to "act" around my male colleagues largely by watching the women around me. I witnessed them slowly shake their head and grin in agreement with others in the room after a male colleague restated an idea they had shared moments before. I heard the click of their designer heels down the hallway and was constantly impressed by their stylish wardrobes while my male colleagues wore jeans, New Balance sneakers, and short-sleeved button-up shirts with a worn hoodie. If a man voiced a somewhat antagonistic point of view, he was seen as a thinker, addressing an issue from all sides. If a woman said something critical, she was seen as difficult.

Psychotherapist and author Sonya Rhodes notes that these dynamics create a catch-22 for professional women. "Whatever women do at work, they have to do it nicely. But the more you back off, the more they don't take you seriously."[2] Women are expected to comply with systems that have cut them down, report to men who have sexualized their appearance and demeaned their personhood, and be so nice it hurts. It's exhausting. It gets a woman nowhere and is a disservice to any space she occupies. More often than not, women tell themselves that they can let low-grade sexism slide *if* they are given a seat or place of power, dignity, and agency. The unspoken understanding is that women have a place in the world not because they deserve it but because a man allowed for them to have a place, and since he has given them opportunities, he holds power over their time, earning potential, and bodies.

This was amplified on a grand scale in the 1940s when America funneled its men abroad during World War II. The government ran a nationwide recruitment campaign, first with posters of glamorous women in the workplace, and then most famously with Rosie the Riveter and her slogan "We Can Do It!" to entice women into joining the civilian and military labor force. It worked. Historians estimate that six million women—of all ethnicities—left their homes or domestic jobs for employment in construction, steel, lumber, agriculture, transportation, government, munitions, and more. They weren't, per se, wanted in these spaces, but they were desperately needed. They were invited by men to fill "men's" roles and endured menial pay, sexual harassment, grueling hours, and less-than-safe working conditions. What was intended to be temporary work, as men would presumably regain their posts once they returned home from war, sparked a revolution of women holding positions in male-dominated spaces across the country and led to collective agency demanding equal rights and protection.[3] Since then, women have continued to pursue positions in male-dominated spaces and fight battles over inequitable power balances.

Interestingly, as Rosie the Riveter stood for a woman's ability and power, another widely recognized World War II image holds an opposing message, yet this message is not as well known. As one of the most acclaimed photos of the twentieth century, the *Unconditional Surrender* photo published in *Life* magazine and later built into a statue standing twenty-six feet tall in Sarasota, Florida, depicts a sailor, George Mendonsa, passionately kissing a nurse, Greta Zimmer Friedman, to celebrate Japan's surrender, marking the end of World War II. Thousands have re-created the iconic kiss, yet the dominant narrative we've come to associate with the piece—that a sailor was so filled with unspeakable joy on VJ Day that he kissed his girl—is dead wrong. Before her death, Friedman explained that the kiss was not consensual. "I did not see him approaching, and before I know it, I was in this vice grip!" Friedman told CBS News in 2012.[4] Mendonsa himself admitted that he had had a few drinks, saw a beautiful woman, grabbed her, and kissed her as world-renowned photographer Alfred Eisenstadt caught the moment on film.[5] Friedman is seen clutching her purse and skirt as a white man in uniform forcibly holds her head in the crook of his arm while he plants a kiss square on her lips. While I doubt either of them thought the moment would be memorialized, the day after Mendonsa died, #MeToo was spray-painted in bold red letters on Friedman's statue leg in Sarasota. What has been romanticized for seventy-five years as a praiseworthy moment in American history, in reality reeks of sexual violence. Historically, in times of need or celebration, women have played the role prescribed to them by those with power.

For marginalized women, the issue of silence is exacerbated by the intersectionality of race, class, and sex.[6] They are less likely to be protected from abusive power and more likely to be silenced and dismissed by their community and the justice system without any recompense for their experiences. Since the time of the transatlantic slave trade, Black female bodies in America have not been their own and have been coerced into sex acts by their slave masters (white men) without punishment. In modern times, Black women are three times as likely as white women to experience sexual harassment at work.[7] Indigenous women are 2.5 times more likely to experience sexual assault and rape than any other ethnic group,[8] and undocumented immigrant low-wage earning women "tend to be placed in situations of greater vulnerability and, through policy, can be denied access to justice," according to the National Network of Immigrant and Refugee Rights.[9] And undocumented immigrants have decreasingly felt safe to report sexual abuse. When Donald Trump became president, reports of rape in Los Angeles by Latina women decreased by 25 percent from January to March 2017, in comparison to the same time frame in 2016. The Los Angeles Police Department attributes this sharp drop in reports to a legitimate fear of deportation.[10] The experiences of women of color are compounded by their race, class, cultural values, and immigration status, leaving them vulnerable in ways not experienced by white women, and despite the undeniable role of racism and classism in sexual misconduct, privileged women largely shape this discussion.

The inconsistent response to abuse of power has played out publicly in recent years by the varied treatment between R. Kelly, Harvey Weinstein, and their sexual abuse victims. R. Kelly's crimes came to light in the summer of 2017, just months before the Weinstein story broke in the *New York Times*. Researchers Rebecca Leung and Robert Williams note that despite credible evidence, testimonies, and well-researched journalism, no charges were brought against R. Kelly after the story broke.[11] According to Chicago-area journalist Jim DeRogatis, Kelly for years maintained a harem of underage girls of color, and his songs continued to stream from major streaming sites all over the world.[12] His victims and accusers were berated for attempting to take down a successful R&B artist and for speaking up against a man from their own community. He had faced charges in the past but was acquitted on all counts. After the 2017 article that exposed his sex cult, Kelly released an eighteen-minute song titled "I Admit." The Weinstein case prompted a different response. Weinstein was forced to step down from his company, lost credibility within the film community, and faced a criminal trial when his heinous actions were publicized. His victims, mostly white women of means and influence, were paraded as heroes, poster women for the #MeToo movement. R. Kelly's victims did not receive the same accolades.[13]

Long before journalists exposed the abuse suffered mostly by white, rich, and famous women, ordinary women who've worked at fast-food chains, hotels, churches, universities, athletic clubs, and elsewhere have attempted to report misconduct at the hands of abusive leaders, yet did not attract the media attention or legal defense that would have highlighted their injustices, let alone prompt lasting institutional change. As bell hooks, Angela Davis, and many other leaders and activists have noted, many Americans are primed to lean in and listen to white women—especially if they have an established platform—while ignoring, downplaying, or ridiculing women of color who speak up. The hierarchy of who will be listened to, who will be believed, who will be silenced, and who will be dismissed has been set, thus far, by the media, the justice system, and patriarchal cultures that have saturated church and state. That must change in order for all women to be protected, supported, and heard. Tarana Burke, founder of the

#MeToo movement, shared in an interview with *Time*, "Sexual violence knows no race, class or gender, but the response to sexual violence absolutely does. Until we change that, any advance that we make in addressing this issue is going to be scarred by the fact that it wasn't across the board."[14] Every woman deserves to be heard, respected, and dignified as she bravely speaks up, not deported, fired, shamed, excommunicated, or worse.

In faith contexts, many good Christian women in well-meaning spaces have been taught that they are the "helpmeet" (Gen. 2:20), which many interpret as an invitation to be meek, obedient, quiet, subservient beings to men, which only perpetuates a patriarchal narrative that can be harmful rather than helpful. The idea that a woman's sole purpose is to *help* goes off the rails when a woman, in the name of God, is expected to emotionally, financially, or even physically bleed simply to meet the demands of the unjust power brokers in her world. No woman should be forced to set herself on fire to keep those who harm her warm. That is not the instruction of the Scriptures, nor does it embody the love of God. Helping as sacrifice is beautiful, but if helping bolsters an imbalance of power, it's no longer helping. It's injustice.

Many women around the world find themselves trapped in unjust systems, where to stay in the room or have a voice—be it in the office, the church, the healthcare system, the country, politics, education, or athletics—they must stick with and defend the one who let them in and must also continuously prove their worth. If the gatekeeper believes they hold less value than a man, they will be treated as such, regardless of the female-friendly ethos of the business, organization, church, or community. What is on paper is not always in practice. When the values etched in stone are not exercised in a consistent and proactive manner, it translates to less pay, less opportunity, and unsafe spaces, and it may be nearly impossible for women to advance in any way, shape, or form, let alone possess a respected voice.

When a woman's livelihood depends on operating in a broken system, she may feel as though she has no choice but to comply. And if the gatekeeper causes her harm by emotional, physical, or sexual harassment, she is forced to deal quietly with the negative social, emotional, and physical consequences for fear that she may lose her income, home, or standing in the community. With so much at risk and few options, she finds herself forcefully corralled into broken systems and unable to rise above them because, more often than not, the power players who are making decisions benefit from the broken system and believe everything *is* just fine. Things do not need to change. This is just the way things are. But everything is just fine only because she holds limited power with no identifiable path to balanced power. Throughout the centuries, this has become the status quo. As author Chimamanda Ngozi Adichie explains, "If we do something over and over, it becomes normal. If we see the same thing over and over, it becomes normal."[15] The power players are not personally hurt, demeaned, demonized, ostracized, harassed, or rejected; therefore, there is no issue. It's only normal.

Sadly, this is not a new dynamic—women subject to the plans of men. We need look no further than the historical accounts in the Bible:

Hagar, forced into surrogacy by her slave masters, Abram and Sarai

Leah, second fiddle to her sister, Rachel

Queen Vashti, summoned to parade in front of drunken party guests

The adulterous woman, dragged into the public square, her business on display

Without agency to harness against the power players of their time, women of the Bible were subjected to the cultural norms, rituals, and humiliation that were both legal and socially acceptable in their day. They were likely familiar with the laws of the land that hindered their safety, security, and well-being, and—barring a few exceptions—they had no political or financial power to fight for rights for themselves or other women. In their day, they could not escape the consequences that came with womanhood. In our day, the systems women combat when they speak up leave them with battle scars. Little do we know how long those scars take to heal when women have been hoodwinked, hushed, and reduced to nothing.

HIS WAY OR THE HIGHWAY

"Who is always looking out for you?"
"You are."
"Who decides if you get paid?"
"You do."
"Who has your best interest at heart?"
"You do."
"Who did God anoint to lead you?"
"You."

The questions always come when the choices he makes are challenged. With low-grade rage, the narcissistic man pitches questions that we most definitely need to answer. In those moments, any hint of insubordination or betrayal is detected and rejected. We are consistently reminded that he holds the power and that it's our job to join him. We are for him or against him; there is no in-between. We convince ourselves that his rage and mood swings are warranted. He has his highs and lows, but so does everyone else. Right? He has more balls to juggle in the air than we do (at least that's what he tells us).

He regularly reminds us how he carries the burden of leading, building, coaching, governing, or teaching, and we do not. He is the one with whom people are always trying to meet, not us. Here is this shiny, turn-your-head-when-he-swaggers-into-the-room, egotistical man who cannot see how he harms. It is dishonorable for someone to question his motive or ways. How dare someone challenge his leadership or ideas. How could anyone usurp his authority? Why would anyone offer anything but respect?

These veiled threats are filtered through defenses that we raise to protect ourselves from his rage. If we are "in" with him, we enjoy the far-reaching influence of his power. We are all ears when he hisses our name from the hallway or when his name lights up on our phone. We know not to ask too many questions, for fear of what would happen if his rage were directed toward us. He is the head of the snake with venom in his bite, although he tries to convince us he is harmless. Even when he coils to attack us, we wonder if defending him to onlookers is necessary. After he slithers away, there is no resolution. Only red marks against *our* actions.

He may have a temper, and by his own admission it is his demon to fight, but doesn't everybody? Doesn't everybody flash their fangs and sink their teeth into flesh when backed into a corner? Our internal excuses on his behalf match those of the people around us, because the fear of him isn't limited only to us—everyone fears his bite. When each attack is more cutting and rage-filled than the last, we do not question. Instead, we know what to do: acknowledge whatever flaw he sees in us, promise to improve, and hope he will not strip us of our power. On occasion, we even thank him for his "honest" feedback.

He balances these attacks with the highest praise, the kindest encouragement, and the eye contact that we crave. Every gnarly episode is matched by a celebrated one where we feel more seen and known by him than anyone else. He knows what we want to hear, and he sings it in our ears at precisely the right time. But the praise and empowerment are all symptoms of something much darker.

It's Not What You Think

It's commonplace to label a seemingly self-centered, power-hungry individual a narcissist, be it a coworker, boss, professor, coach, president, Hollywood producer, partner, or friend. The term is known well enough that we label just about anyone a narcissist if they post too many selfies on social media, waiting for applause in the form of "likes" as a measure of self-worth. While snapping pics of duck lips and avocado toast may not qualify someone as a narcissist, those who are interested only in advancing their own agenda and who appear aggressive seem to fit the bill. Yet there is more than meets the eye when it comes to narcissists and their ability to abuse their power. Narcissists do not lack the persuasion and charm needed to get ahead. In reality, they are experts at employing their persona to get what they want—or who they want—when they want it.

According to the *Diagnostic and Statistical Manual of Mental Disorders,* the authoritative text on mental health and personality disorders, those with diagnosable narcissistic personality disorder struggle with major impairments in interpersonal functioning. Relationships are largely superficial and exist to serve self-esteem regulation. They also struggle to recognize or identify with the feelings and needs of others.[1]

"Narcissism plays out in the idea that they are owed something, in the idea that they are entitled to their authority, that their partners have to be subservient to them."[2] This reduces nearly every interpersonal relationship to a shallow one that exists only to serve the narcissist. The toxic combination of narcissism, sexism, and discrimination within systems predates first- and second-wave women's movements, and the term *sexual harassment* didn't even exist until the late seventies, despite decades-long denigration of working women. As women entered previously male-dominated workspaces, men frequently conditioned women's employment opportunities on compliance with male sexual advances. Moreover, environments were polluted with pornographic material, demeaning language, and sexist insults.[3] With a heritage of flaunted dominance, narcissistic men exploited power dynamics to stalk their prey.

Power Dynamics

In an interview for *Berkeley Scientific Journal*, psychologist Dacher Keltner is reported as saying, "People in power often are able to say what they want and take what they desire. However, people who do not have power feel constrained in various aspects. People in lower power feel a greater threat, have higher cortisol levels, greater sympathetic autonomic nervous system activation, and greater blood pressure. Their minds are more inhibited; when they speak, they hesitate, interrupt themselves, and [do] not say what they actually think."[4] Power clearly affects how one thinks and behaves. When narcissists employ their strengths, financial assets, industry connections, and position to seek a seat of power and remain in power, they wield weapons from their arsenal to stay seated in a place of power while they inflict emotional and psychological abuse on their prey. We live in a world that all but worships powerful people, and narcissists see themselves seated on the throne of a dysfunctional structure.

After twenty years of silence, Rowena Chiu, who in her early twenties was an assistant to the once-powerful Hollywood producer Harvey Weinstein, came forward to tell her harrowing story of sexual assault to the *New York Times*. She explained how her power-hungry boss took advantage of complex power dynamics to trap her into his sick cycle of abuse. Chiu writes,

> Harvey played games . . . testing how far he could go, wielding both the carrot (if you survived working with him, he could make your career) and the stick (if you refused his advances, he would do his best to ensure you never again worked in the movie industry).
>
> I've had many years to ruminate on how I fell into Harvey's trap, and the best way to understand it is through the four power dynamics of gender, race, seniority and wealth.
>
> The first power imbalance—that of man versus woman—was obvious. I was a woman in an industry in which women still struggle to be taken seriously. Harvey was a man in an industry in which men dominate, and he often used that dominance to claim sexual favors.
>
> The second power imbalance was around race—the fact that Harvey was white and I was a person of color. My ethnicity initially marked me as different and inferior: He assured Zelda [her supervisor] that he wouldn't harass me because he didn't, as I remember it, "do Chinese or Jewish girls." Then later, he turned around and defined me in terms of sexual exoticism, telling me, just before he tried to rape me, that he'd never had a Chinese girl.
>
> The third power imbalance was around seniority. Harvey was a power player, and I was the lowest person on the totem pole. Assistants are the unseen work force that props Hollywood up, and yet we have zero leverage. I was invisible and inconsequential.
>
> Finally, the wealth—Harvey was a multimillionaire, with all the influence money could buy. I was a fresh graduate loaded with student debt. Even during the few months I worked with him, I saw firsthand the influence that money could buy. Later, I was to discover that it could even buy silence.[5]

Chiu perfectly outlines the varied power dynamics that were present in her experience with Weinstein, and in doing so,

uncovers the power dynamics present in systems we all find ourselves in. For Chiu, who signed a nondisclosure agreement that
barred her from speaking about what happened with her pastor, therapist, and even her future husband, attempted suicide
twice before leaving Miramax, Weinstein's company. According
to Chiu's *New York Times* essay, Weinstein's gross abuse of power
eventually left her unemployable and fighting the traumatic
effects of working for an abusive boss long after she left.[6]

Narcissists, no matter what system they work their way into,
are aware of what works and what doesn't to get what they
want. They will easily manipulate those involved so eventually
everything bends their way. They will exploit an imbalance of
power to move in on the prey that will, in their mind, feed
their ego and desires. Many women who are preyed upon don't
easily spot the power imbalances, which is why they often feel
that they are to blame for any and all fallout. Only after wise
counsel and time to recover from their experience are many
victims able to see with clarity that what happened to them
was at the hands of an experienced manipulator who did not
hesitate to abuse his power.

Love Bombing

As Shahida Arabi, author and mental health practitioner,
notes, "What makes narcissistic abuse so dangerous is that
these individuals employ covert and insidious methods to
abuse their partners. Due to the very nature of their abuse,
they're able to escape accountability for the abuse because of
the false persona they present to the outside world—which is
usually a charming mask that hides their cruelty."[7]

While an abuser of power might be your employer or spiritual leader and not your partner in the way that Arabi describes, patterns of "love bombing" can still be identified as
over the top. Love bombing is the practice of a narcissist or

manipulator showering another with affection, gifts, and promises for the future in an attempt to control the other person.[8] For those being love bombed, it can feel like discovering a kindred soul who sees our true worth, or the narcissist could present himself as a dream boss showering down opportunities that most are given only after years of experience.

Those who employ love bombing text or call excessively, demand ample periods of time, and choose what happens when they are together. While that might be easy to spot in a romantic relationship that moves too quickly, it's not as easy to spot with an enthusiastic boss, coach, professor, or other leader who is taking advantage of his place. If a woman recently landed a job, role, or position that she expected to run successfully, she might never question the excessive contact her superior demands she give.

Love bombing quickly backfires whenever the target does not give in to, have time for, or agree with the narcissist. When she overtly or subtly makes herself unavailable to meet the benchmarks the narcissist puts into place, her time will be up. She will likely fall out of right standing so quickly that she'll wonder where *she* messed up. Even more, if other targets of the narcissist surround her, she may wonder why they still have all the love and opportunity in the world while she is left on the outside looking in. Narcissists easily devalue relationships that no longer serve them as they likely have a pipeline of new supply who are happy to bend over backward and serve as the apple of the narcissist's eye.

Like a falling stock, a woman's credibility can be tanked by a narcissist so fast she's left grappling for any resemblance of her former life, *or* it can be a quiet decline with off-handed comments and loss of power. Narcissists may start a whisper campaign to convince others she is unruly, opinionated, jealous, and insecure. She may be barred from future opportunities, demoted, or the topic of damning gossip. Whatever it is she values (position, credibility, work opportunities, interpersonal relationships), that is likely what the narcissist will look to steal, until she is left feeling destroyed, in a no-win situation through no fault of her own. She may dust herself off and attempt to get back in his good graces, even willing to ignore her convictions to meet the absurd emotional, mental, and sexual needs of the narcissist, especially if she feels she owes him for his attention. She may feel as though the rejection is her responsibility and she could never tell anyone of the ill behavior since she believes she put herself in harm's way.

She fears that every life choice she makes for her own well-being could be a mark against her from *him*, the very one she's trying to please. She may fall in love with someone that is not the abusive manipulator in her life, or she might refuse to answer every single phone call from him or make herself generally unavailable as she prioritizes her sanity. She may stand her ground one too many times and lose her credibility in the office. Just a few wrong moves in the chess game that she's bound to lose, and she'll be stripped of her golden-girl status. She might not be able to pinpoint the moment she lost her credibility, but she can vividly remember feeling that there was no way she would ever regain the influence she once had. He took away opportunities that she will never recover. Even worse, he'll tell others before she will ever know.

After her swift kick to the curb, the edges of her world slowly fray. Where she once had good rapport with those in the system, where her opinion and insight were valued, she is now ignored. Where she once was included, she is now on the outside looking in.

In her heart of hearts, she knew the day would come when her number would be up. She'd seen several others come and go, quickly in and out of his favor, and it was only a matter of time until it would be her who was kicked out of the club. Meanwhile, for each new woman in his life, just as attractive, bright, and capable as the last, he will idolize her and give her opportunity as long as she keeps to his pace and preferences. This cycle of manipulation and shame happens everywhere and anywhere narcissists find their way to the top.

Narcissists don't prey only on insecure women. Their charisma can fool the most educated, emotionally healthy, accomplished woman. Every woman is fair game to the narcissist as long as she meets his needs and makes him feel as though he is the one who holds the power and deserves the applause.

If the woman hooked by the narcissist wants to escape the web of narcissism before he is ready to discard her, he will love bomb her once more, and this time, zero reconnaissance work on what she values or wants is necessary because he already knows. He will shower her with love, affection, and gifts, often claiming she is the only one who understands him. She gets him, and what they share is priceless. In those situations, where she is adored and doted on, it's easy to engage in euphoric recall, where she looks back on her experiences only in a positive light.[9] She remembers his version of the story, leaving the true and toxic experience in the recesses of her mind.

Addressing the Narcissist

If their bizarre and harmful behavior is addressed, narcissists can whip out a heartfelt apology and compassionate response if they've trained themselves to do so, even asking if the other person has ever felt the way they are being accused of. If necessary, they can flash their brokenness and humanity to those questioning them just enough to be believable, and squelch any disbelief in their ability to conduct themselves with anything but maximum respect and empathy. Their false sense of humility, coupled with their dazzling charm, makes for a quick escape from any accusation of wrongdoing. This is perhaps best displayed in faith settings.

Chuck DeGroat, professor of pastoral care and Christian spirituality at Western Theological Seminary, observes,

> A shallow view of sin leads to a shallow repentance. Shallow repentance looks like admitting the troubling behavior and committing to not doing it again—case closed. And thus, shallow repentance leads to quick restoration. After all, who wouldn't believe the sincerity of a pastor who preaches so wonderfully and charismatically, and who has influenced so many? Shallow repentance can look like blame dressed in the garments of personal responsibility—"I'm really sorry that hurt you." Shallow repentance can also look "raw and honest," at times. It can be accompanied by words that seem spiritual—"Saul lifted up his voice and wept . . . I have sinned" (see 1 Sam 24; Matt. 7:3). But it's another manifestation of narcissism's grandiosity and incapacity to connect with the true self. It is repentance as self-preservation, not as confession "with grief and hatred of one's sin," as the old Puritan once put it. And narcissists do this really well! Even more, shallow repentance only repents of the above-the-waterline behaviors, for looking beneath is harder, more timely, and would likely reveal a depth of deceit within that he doesn't want to see.[10]

Christian subculture invites a softer, more rehearsed response from narcissists or their public-relations teams. Yet in most cases, narcissists will lose their ever-loving minds if anyone speaks up and will make their challenger wish they had held their tongue. As clinical psychologist Leon F. Seltzer explains, "If you directly confront a malignant narcissist, you'll never succeed in puncturing their ironclad defenses. Plus, they're notorious for counter-punching really, really hard. . . . Even a simple suggestion that they try doing something differently can make them bare their teeth at you, cobra-like. It doesn't take long for most people dealing with narcissists to realize they don't take criticism well, if at all."[11]

Worn and tired from mind games, coercive control, and the tendency to gaslight her, a woman can feel doomed by her encounters with a narcissistic power abuser.

She is doomed if she stays.

She is doomed if she is discarded.

She is doomed if she addresses it.

She is doomed if she tries to escape.

Not only does she feel hopeless, a woman's participation with a narcissist leaves her with a twisted sense of culpability. She isn't innocent. She ate up the praise, accepted the gifts, and took the opportunities. He likely has the receipts. His distorted idolization drew her in, and she feels some level of responsibility and guilt for what has happened. There is nothing quite as convincing as guilt to silence a woman from speaking up about her experience.

The way that a narcissist silences women is, in some ways, dictated by how much she believes his interpretation of the ordeal. Which, after the coercive abuse of a narcissist, is hard to understand without his spin on it. An easy way to silence a woman is to convince her that the experience never happened in the first place, that she misunderstood his intentions, or, my personal favorite, that she is seeing things that aren't really there.

For most women who are engaged in any sort of relationship with a narcissist, there appears to be no resolution, unless she is willing to believe *his* flawed telling of events. Due to the psychological harm a woman endures, it's uncomplicated to believe she is the one who is crazy, incapable, insecure, too sensitive, broken, and damaged, and so admit that she did this to herself. It is in her best interest to stay silent since she's the train wreck in the situation. At least that's what he tells her.

Until the Supreme Court says otherwise. Perhaps one of the most famous cases of sexist narcissism at work was the experience of Mechelle Vinson, a bank teller who was sexually violated by her branch manager, Sidney L. Taylor, in the seventies. Vinson was hired at nineteen and claimed that Taylor, a deacon at his church, married man, and father of seven children, waited only a few months before coercing her into bed. When Vinson resisted Taylor's insistence on sleeping with her, he replied, "Just like I hired you, I'll fire you. Just like I made you, I'll break you, and if you don't do what I say then I'll have you killed." For four years Vinson was subject to harassment, often in front of her coworkers. Vinson was forcibly raped by Taylor on several occasions, even once while trapped inside a bank vault. In an interview with the *Washington Post*, she confessed how degrading Taylor was. "We would have problems with the air conditioning and he would say, 'Mechelle, go downstairs and check the air conditioning,' and I would go, and he would come down, grab me," she said. "It was just something like, you're an animal, you're nothing, and I'm going to show you you're nothing." After Vinson rose to the position of assistant branch manager, and had endured assault an estimated forty times, she took a leave of absence and was fired.

Once Vinson lost her job, she sued Taylor and the bank. Her case made it to a US district judge, who ruled in the bank's favor, claiming that employers were liable only if they were made aware of the harassment and refused to rectify the situation. Vinson appealed and the decision was reversed. The bank then appealed, which led the case to be heard before the Supreme Court. In a unanimous ruling on June 19, 1986, eight years after Vinson first sued Taylor and the bank, sexual harassment was deemed a violation of federal law, and companies could be held liable for harassment committed by leadership—regardless of whether the company was aware of violations.[12]

Narcissistic sexual abuse by powerful men in the workplace, from that day on, had consequences that reverberated around the country, because according to the laws of the land, it was considered discrimination and, therefore, illegal. In the following ten years, as more high-profile cases were brought to national attention, sexual harassment cases reported to the Equal Employment Opportunity Commission (the government organization tasked with investigating workplace misconduct) skyrocketed as women bravely stood up to powerful men preying on them.[13] Yet, for many women throughout the last thirty years, silence still seemingly remains the best option.

3

BE QUIET

Years before I ever uttered the phrase "Time's Up" alongside the collective voice of hundreds of thousands of women across the country, I sat on my bathroom floor paralyzed with fear, sweat seeping through my pajamas. Like others with a secret, I felt my heart race and my stomach churn, and I struggled with debilitating anxiety, restless sleep, and horrid nightmares. My husband was fast asleep while I lay on the cold tile, tortured by my own thoughts. Question after question left me more anxious than the one before. I thought to myself, *What do I do? Whom do I tell? Will anyone listen?* But by the next morning, I vowed to myself that I would swallow the truth like a horse pill and be quiet. *If I'm quiet, they can't attack. If I'm quiet, they can't shame me. If I'm quiet, they can't destroy me.* In my mind, my ironclad excuses would protect not only me, I reasoned, but also the other women in my world.

Many of us aren't the girl or boy who cried wolf. We haven't done, in our estimation, anything worthy of losing credibility, but we know that if we speak truth to power, we'll face dire consequences. We'll be painted as a person we are not, nothing but a liar. On a power trip. Jealous. In reality, we are none of those things. We are people who fear the wrath of patriarchal power. We're convinced our silence will protect us. We talk ourselves out of bravery, because surely we can get by without whispering a word to anyone. We drink the poison of silent suffering and hope to escape the chaos.

But how will we live with the secret? A secret that leaves us anxious, depressed, sick, and isolated. Haunting us at night and hounding us in the day.

Secrets

In our right mind, none of us would share anything that would invite harm on ourselves or the people we care for. Many of us would rather live with secrets than find out what happens if we tell the truth—because we know the consequences are different for everyone. Many of us, myself included, didn't learn this as adults who had seen some things—we learned this before we could even spell our name. From a young age, I feared being branded as broken, shameful, or a troublemaker. Without language to process my own experiences, or an understanding of the effects of secret keeping, I convinced myself that I couldn't afford the high cost of truth telling despite what I had witnessed or experienced. In observational research by psychologists studying secrecy in childhood, children even as young as twenty-four months are capable of lying,[1] and they will downplay the harmful acts of others.[2] In addition, young children will agree to conceal the inappropriate acts of those who care for them.[3]

As adults, no matter how we end up with a secret, many of us keep the secret, even to our detriment. Secrets, in our minds, keep the peace. They prevent change. We feel a false sense of power by keeping them and fail to realize that we don't actually keep secrets—secrets keep us. Some shameful secrets make us feel small, worthless, and powerless. If we feel guilt, we wade through feelings of remorse, tension, and regret.[4] Secrets can cause us to be hypervigilant, paranoid, and anxious in ways that keep us enslaved to the shameful truth of what we know, or have seen, or have done. We feel trapped with no painless escape in sight.

Michael Slepian, professor at Columbia Business School, says this of secrets:

> It hurts to keep secrets. Secrecy is associated with lower well being, worse health, and less satisfying relationships. Research has linked secrecy to increased anxiety, depression, symptoms of poor health, and even the more rapid progression of disease. There is a seemingly obvious explanation for these harms: Hiding secrets is hard work. You have to watch what you say. If asked about something related to the secret, you must be careful not to slip up. This could require evasion or even deception. Constant vigilance and concealment can be exhausting.
>
> New research, however, suggests that the harm of secrets doesn't really come from the hiding after all. The real problem with keeping a secret is not that you have to hide it, but that you have to live with it, and think about it.[5]

As evidenced from Slepian's research, secrets have a profound effect on our well-being, and living with secrets becomes a burden to bear. However, secret-keeping may feel like the safest option when we quietly watch women from a safe distance publicly tell their secret only to be censured for their bravery. They pay a price, often in the public square, that warns other women what will happen if they muster up the courage to tell of their experience. Few women who have publicly spoken up in the last few years know this better than Dr. Christine Blasey Ford.

According to Ford's testimony before Congress, she was in high school when two drunk teenage boys corralled her into a bedroom at a party. Ford alleges that US Supreme Court nominee Brett Kavanaugh pinned her to a bed, groping her as he attempted to strip off her clothes and smothered her screams for help. After Kavanaugh's friend jumped on top of them and they fell to the floor, she said, she escaped to a nearby bathroom, locked the door, and then fled the home after she heard the boys stumble down the stairs. She never told another soul of the details until she sat in couple's counseling with her husband in 2012.

For Kavanaugh, a lifetime appointment to the Supreme Court was in jeopardy. In October 2018, over twenty million people watched Ford answer questions left, right, and center from senators.[6] She remembered the best she could obscure details from a nightmarish encounter, as Kavanaugh hot-headedly denied every bit of Ford's traumatic experience, one that she had spent years seeking treatment for. In the end, "the hopes and fears of women and men who have lived with the trauma of sexual violence were riding on the credibility of Ford's testimony. Her treatment in the halls of power, and her reception by an expectant public, would send a signal to countless survivors wrestling with whether they should speak up."[7]

Ford initially didn't intend to share her story of assault with the world, as she assumed it would bear no consequence as to whether Kavanaugh would be confirmed to the court, but she rightly assumed it would destroy her life. Yet, after a confidential letter to a senior lawmaker intended only to be in Kavanaugh's background file was leaked without her consent, journalists discovered her identity and swarmed her house and workplace, and inaccuracies ran rampant about the kind of woman she was and what happened decades before. After her identity was revealed, she felt that her civic responsibility outweighed her anguish and terror about retaliation. Ford told of her experience before the judiciary committee, reliving every moment of her attack.

Before her name was plastered on every news site or trending on social media, Ford passed a polygraph test conducted by a former FBI agent when detailing her account, at the urging of her lawyer, famed victims' rights attorney Debra Katz.[8] But as Ford sat on the stand, answering questions from lawmakers about a horrific night that took place over three decades before, she was fuzzy on time and details, as often happens in cases of trauma, which she explained herself as an accomplished psychology professor.[9] As her long-held secret became the hot topic of public discourse, her words were twisted and her story was politicized.

Despite her testimony, the world watched as Kavanaugh was confirmed to the Supreme Court while Ford faced threats of the worst kind. Her personal information, including her home address, was posted online. She and her family moved at least four times to ensure their safety. She and her husband hired a private security detail to protect them as the death threats ensued.[10] The consequences of speaking up and telling her story were painfully high. Regardless of whether we believe that Ford rightly remembered the events from thirty-plus years ago and whether Kavanaugh was her actual assaulter, no woman should fear for her life for coming forward with a story of being violated. Not one.

As women around the world watched what happened to a woman coming forward after years of silence, and President Donald Trump questioned her credibility, saying that if the attack "was as bad as she says," she or her parents would have reported it to the authorities when it happened, the hashtag #WhyIDidntReport flooded newsfeeds.[11] Women from all walks of life shared honestly about why they didn't go to police or other authorities over the crimes or violations against them when they initially took place. For many, they believed it was their fault and therefore their duty to stay silent. For others, the person who assaulted them ensured that their lives would be ruined if they ever spoke up.

- "He told me it was my fault, and I believed him."[12]
- "He was 6 ft and I'm 5'3". I'm scared he would hurt me if I did."[13]
- "Because I was 6 years old. Because he was suppose to be 'family.' Because I convinced myself for 14 years that it was a morbid dream I had when I was little."[14]
- "I was 10, in the back of a church bus and had absolutely no idea what was happening."[15]
- "He was my mum's boyfriend and she had just lost my dad after 30 years of marriage, I didn't want to hurt her or be the reason she lost someone else."[16]
- "I was 10, he was my stepdad and said he would hurt my mom if I did. But once he did something to my sister who was 5 YEARS OLD I finally got the courage to speak up about my sister but not about myself."[17]
- "Because people told me not to ruin his life and reputation, as if his punishment was more severe than mine."[18]
- "He knew where my entire family lived and threatened to harm them in any way possible."[19]

For many women, keeping secrets to conceal the truth appears to be the only—torturous—option when they feel it was their fault, their reputation is on the line, or their pocketbook depends on it. "It's scary for anybody," Emily Martin, vice president for workplace justice at the National Women's Law Center explains, "but it's especially threatening if you don't have a financial cushion and your paycheck is the only thing standing between your family and homelessness."[20] Like when a farmworker was raped by her boss and then told that she should remember the reason she even had a job was because of him. Another woman had her breasts and buttocks repeatedly groped by her supervisor as she picked onions and potatoes. He told her that if she resisted he would call immigration.[21] Women from all walks of life stay silent long after their harassment and assault for fear of their own fate. Even after they become a psychology professor in Silicon Valley.

Yet for many women, if they weren't silenced by fear, guilt, or shame, money muzzles them.

Nondisclosure Agreements

Grade-school girls suffer at the hands of playground ruffians. High-school girls silently endure cyber bullying. College girls are discouraged from reporting rape on campuses so as not to sully the image of the institution. Women hide bruises and scars given to them by boyfriends and husbands. Working women refuse to report humiliation and harassment to human resources. They either choose to stay silent or are silenced by power players, but, most of all, women refuse to subject themselves to character annihilation or public backlash. Many times, they are compensated for their silence.

Those looking to silence a woman's testimony can often accomplish this if they offer to pay up. Women are offered hush money contingent on a signed nondisclosure agreement (NDA) from those with power and a reputation to protect. If a person in power is unwilling to lose his power at the expense of a woman with a story to tell and is willing to pay a price to keep a secret, then that's exactly what he will do. Powerful men from every sector—corporate America, church, politics, education, athletics—crack open the checkbook to make their problems go away.

Writing for *Harvard Business Review*, law professor Orly Lobel notes that NDAs "not only appear in settlements after a victim of sexual harassment has raised her voice but also are now routinely included in standard employment contracts upon hiring. At the outset, NDAs attempt to impose several obligations upon a new employee. They demand silence, often broadly worded to protect against speaking up against corporate culture or saying anything that would portray the company and its executives in a negative light."[22]

Regardless of the injustice that occurred, NDAs ultimately provide protection not for the one harmed but for the one who harms. "NDAs are enormously controversial, even within the legal community," writes Michelle Dean in the *Columbia Journalism Review*. "From one vantage—say that of an exceptionally cautious lawyer, or an exceptionally frightened employee—keeping silent is thought necessary to avoid hefty financial penalties."[23] In some cases, companies will use threats and intimidation—for example, by insinuating that a woman has been promiscuous or insubordinate—in order to coerce them into signing an NDA. For fear of losing gold stars, or her potential to advance in her career, or to keep her place in her church and community, she'll sign her silence on the dotted line.

"The system works against victims in other ways too: Litigation is costly, stressful, and frequently prohibits or otherwise prevents a litigant from obtaining new employment," writes Diana Falzone for *Vanity Fair*. "In the post-#MeToo era, these settlement agreements are a relic of a system designed to prevent women from telling their own stories or to correct falsehoods disseminated by former employees or their surrogates."[24] The alarming reality is that a woman can apply for a job in a complicit workplace, one that appears to be a winning and supportive space for women, and have no clue of the dangers that await her, because every woman before her who was victimized has been censored from sharing her experience. She might be walking into a lions' den without a warning that she may be devoured.

"Michele Landis Dauber, a professor at Stanford Law School, noted that 'silence is pretty much the only thing the victim has to bargain with.' Still, she said, there was a greater good in banning NDAs. 'These agreements are not in the public interest because they allow for serial harassers to continue to inflict damage on multiple people down the road,' she said."[25]

Last, if a victimized woman chooses to pursue legal action against an abuser, she could spend years in court and still lose her case or be stuck with legal fees that exceed a settlement offer. Without hard evidence, documented misconduct, and solid corroboration, it's difficult to win a case in criminal or civil court against a person in power who has the necessary arsenal to destroy a woman's testimony as he defends his position. Her legal representation may push her to accept an NDA with a financial settlement, as it guarantees a quick payday for her attorney. In other words, it's a profitable business for law firms to negotiate NDAs contingent on financial settlements, with some firms charging as much as 40 percent of the final payout.[26]

The silence is damaging to the woman whose adverse experiences leave her with a lump of cash but no real sense that any sort of justice has been served. Any woman who has experienced shame, assault, humiliation, isolation, rejection, harassment, or abuse, and has agreed to strictly enforced silence, forbidden to share her experience with family, friends, therapists, and mentors, is left to cope with the grievous repercussions on her own.

Tamar

As followers of Jesus, we find ourselves reflected in the men and women of biblical times, the victorious and the victimized. We see ourselves in their actions, their pain, and their terror. Although modern women enjoy freedoms that would be unthinkable in previous generations, they are intimately familiar with the vulnerability of the women who've gone before them, and not just in the shiny accounts of the Proverbs 31 woman, Mary, and Deborah. They find themselves in Tamar too.

A story from what Phyllis Trible refers to as the "texts of terror"[27] is the experience of Tamar, daughter of King David, which leaves readers feeling hungry for justice. As her half-brother and cousin plot her sexual assault, it seems as though Tamar is not a woman to respect or care for but a woman to be conquered because Amnon "fell desperately in love with her" (2 Sam. 13:1 NLT). Once trapped in her brother's room, Tamar pleads for her safety, but Amnon refuses to listen and rapes her. After Amnon's selfish, vile crime against Tamar, his love twists into hate, and he throws her out. Not once do we read of Tamar's concern or consent—only her cries for mercy. She is left alone to tear her virgin robe.

After the incident, her brother Absalom encourages her to stay silent. "Don't you worry about it," he says (2 Sam. 13:20 NLT).[28] The man whom she likely feels closest to tells her to be quiet—to keep her pain to herself and suffer in silence. Her father, the man after God's own heart, is *angry* over the matter. We aren't presented with any evidence that King David punishes Amnon or denounces his heinous actions. We aren't offered any words of compassion or comfort he might sing over his daughter. Only speechless fury. Popular Bible teacher Jen Wilkin says this of the text: "David sacrificed Bathsheba to his lust and then murdered her husband to cover his tracks. Now his two sons fulfill God's prophecy of judgment by committing heightened versions of his own sins within their own family. David's guilt renders him silent. Tamar's plea to Amnon as he overpowers her rings in the ears of the reader: *As for me, where could I carry my shame?* And David's profound silence gives us our answer: *Nowhere.*"[29]

As women are silenced, their story does not vanish into thin air; it simply goes underground. Every woman who has been silenced eventually comes to the realization that just because she doesn't talk about it doesn't mean she can go on as if it didn't happen. I'm not referring only to sexual misconduct that goes unreported. Women are silenced by teachers who think STEM fields are for the boys, by professors who think women have no business speaking up, by coaches who think women are weak and can be mastered, by pastors who think women should shut up and look pretty, by doctors who think women have no idea what they are talking about, by bosses who assume their female colleagues should take the notes and get the coffee, and by the coworkers who simply watch as women do just that. And how many girls have learned silence from their own fathers and mothers who don't want anyone to know what's happened under their roof?

If women are trained to be silent from their life experiences, their conditioned response is likely to affect their view of God, of others, and of themselves. They subconsciously know their place in the world by the way others treat them. They may nurse their wounds in private, but what if they didn't have to? What if we could hold space for women who have been harmed, who have been humiliated, and who have been silenced? Lament alongside them? Ensure them that they are seen, that their stories matter, and that they will be treated with the utmost care? What if our churches, kitchen tables, and faith gatherings were the safest of places for them to process those experiences? What if silence weren't spiritual? What if we not only listened but also committed to the process of healing? Of wholeness?

As someone who has grown up in church, I find it interesting that we are quick to parade a woman onstage, or share her story on social media, only if she has *already* overcome; we might even share the salacious tidbits that will really get folks salivating. We ask her to tell her story, or a pastor tells it

57

from his point of view, inadvertently forcing her to relive the trauma. But for the woman who has yet to harness her story and wrangle it into something shiny and beautiful—well, we don't always know what to do with those. Those are the ones we silence because their story requires changes that have yet to be made, hard conversations we aren't willing to have, and healing that we haven't made time for. We must not only celebrate the woman who has overcome, but we must make space for all women to overcome.

To right the cultural wrong of silencing women, we must be ready to listen to whatever a woman might confide in us. It could be far outside the lines of what we believe is acceptable, and our trite comebacks, our disapproving nods, and our willingness to write her off as "needy" are far from helpful. Her story must do more than anger us. We mustn't fall mute when we feel uncomfortable or infuriated by her experience. Her pain is our pain. Her brokenness is our brokenness. If she has been harmed, silenced, and taken advantage of, so have we. If we want her to speak up, we must go first.

We must be willing to talk about the atrocities that happen against women and make it plain that there is no room for such behavior, and that we will not sit silently while our sisters, mothers, and daughters endure unthinkable tragedy. We are strongest when we carry our desolate sister to the throne of God, refuse to leave, and serve as an active ally in her resurrection. Although Tamar's voice was not heard, may we give a voice to the women of our time until the day we see our Advocate, the one who exchanges our shame for grace. Even if it costs us more social equity than we thought we could afford.

4

BUT HE'S DONE SO MUCH FOR ME

We don't want him to get hurt, we tell ourselves. We rationalize that the offender certainly acted below reproach but ultimately is a good man, right? He was the one who listened to our complaints. He was the one who reminded us on our darkest days that the dawn was sure to come. He lobbied for our advancement and promoted us. He led us in the sinner's prayer and treated us with the grace we so desperately craved. We owe him our allegiance.

We do not wish for him to face the consequences of his actions, because we fear not only what he would do to us if he knew we stood as an accuser of his wrongdoing but also because he has positioned himself as a supporter in our lives and promoter of our gifts. He has done so much for us. We may resonate with the sentiments of Nancy Beach, former teaching pastor at Willow Creek Community Church, when she told the *Chicago Tribune* of her own experience with charismatic leader Bill Hybels: "He changed my life. I wouldn't have the opportunities I've had. I know that. I'm very clear on that. I credit him for that. But then there's this other side."[1]

We grapple with how the offender has upended our life, and the lives of others, while at the same time he propelled our journey to heights no one else had. We certainly don't see it as our responsibility to drum up courage to tell the truth. That is not our predicament. Our real quandary is that we fear betraying him—the boss, coach, mentor, spiritual leader, professor, or father figure. We couldn't possibly commit treason against the man who has committed himself to the advancement of our personal, professional, and spiritual lives.

We ask ourselves, "Could someone else find out the nature of his actions and report him? Could someone else tell the truth and expose his duplicitous ways? Could someone else hope to withstand the wrath of his brutal attacks if listed as a named accuser? Does it have to be us? Could it be someone who wasn't paid by him? Someone whose retirement account wasn't dependent upon his empire? Someone who didn't enjoy working at his organization? Someone who didn't feel a dutiful obligation to protect him? Maybe they should speak up. They should shoulder the burden of this mess. Not us. He's done so much for us."

What are we to do when our loyalty to him is juxtaposed with our convictions? We know that what he's doing, or did, is indisputably wrong, but how can we afford to lose our relationship with a man who has made a way for us? How can we put him through any sort of investigation? The more we ponder his kindness toward us, the more we make excuses for him. Even though he's likely strung us along to such a rotten place of loyalty that he's counting on our silence if he's ever found out, we conclude that we could not betray him, nor could we betray the system he represents. We believe that since he deeply cares for us—compared to what happens in high-profile, celebrity relationships—surely it isn't that bad.

You Don't Really Know Him

When Janay Palmer chose to stay with NFL running back Ray Rice after security camera footage documented Rice beating Palmer unconscious in an elevator in Atlantic City, many women, including myself, were bewildered—but not all. Some intimately understood and identified with her and posted on social media their own stories of why they stayed with their abusers. Here is a report of what one woman wrote on Twitter: "'I tried to leave the house once after an abusive episode, and he blocked me,' she wrote about her ex-partner, adding the hashtag #whyistayed. 'I thought that love would conquer all,' she added in a subsequent message. Other domestic violence survivors picked up the hashtag and offered their own reasons for staying with men who had made them suffer."[2]

Not only did Palmer stay with him after footage leaked of the abuse, she fiercely defended her man and claimed the video was taken out of context. Rice was indicted on an assault charge that carried a potential jail sentence of three to five years. As *New York Times* reporter Jodi Kantor notes, "Testifying against Mr. Rice would have meant ending his football career, embarrassing the team and possibly sending her daughter's father to jail. Instead, Janay Palmer married him the day after the indictment."[3]

In a press conference not long after the indictment, Palmer (now Rice) shared,

I do deeply regret the role that I played in the incident that night, but I can say that I am happy that we continue to work through it together, and we are continuing to strengthen our relationship and our marriage and do what we have to do for not only ourselves collectively, but individually, and working on being better parents for Rayven and continue to be good role models for the community like we were doing before this. I love Ray, and I know that he will continue to prove himself to not only you all, but [to] the community, and I know he will gain your respect back in due time. So thank you.[4]

She claimed a level of responsibility for the abuse and made a public commitment to Rice: the father of her child, her spouse, and the man whom the world witnessed beat her unconscious and spit on her body. The stance that she has chosen to share with the public is that of a loyal supporter—whether he deserves it or not. He is, after all, the one who took care of her.

Many women who find themselves dependent on a man who abuses his power—whether it is a spouse who provides for the partnership, a boss who signs the paychecks, or a professor who holds the grades needed for an academic scholarship—slip into a cycle of abuse that garners empathy for the abuser. This form of silence is reliant on conditioning the abused woman to make excuses for the abuser at her own expense. When you ask a woman who has, at some point, felt loved and cared for by her abuser, she is likely to forgive the repeated misconduct no matter how trivial or severe.

As confused as many of us may be by Janay Palmer's choice to stand by her man, we do the same if we make excuses for men who exploit our loyalty. We act against our own intuition, and after repeat behavior, we tell ourselves, *he's done so much for me*. That's what happens in a toxic culture; your conscience is methodically eroded over time by someone else's negative or inappropriate words or actions.

Corporate Stockholm Syndrome

A cocktail of manipulation, rejection, and altruism is sipped by a woman whose livelihood depends on working in a compromised environment and dulls her emotional and mental senses. If she remains on a steady diet of maltreatment *and* generosity served by the same leader without intervention, over time her view of him will likely be astonishingly skewed. At best, she may assume he's a kind, good-hearted man with a somewhat flawed character. At worst, she will be his faithful defender no matter what sins he's committed.

Psychotherapist James Ullrich notes that, because so much of our self-worth in the modern world is defined by and derived from work, we are at risk of Corporate Stockholm Syndrome when put into a certain professional environment for long enough. Corporate Stockholm Syndrome can be defined as employees of a business beginning to identify with—and being deeply loyal to—an employer who mistreats them (defined in this situation as verbal abuse, demanding overly long hours, and generally ignoring the well-being and emotional needs of the employee). As with the captor/captive dynamic in the traditional understanding of Stockholm Syndrome, the employer is certainly in control of the employee's fate (they sign the much-needed paycheck and generally can terminate employment at any time).

An employee with Corporate Stockholm Syndrome typically displays a tendency to become attached to the company to the detriment of their emotional health. The employee will rationalize to themselves and others the employer's poor treatment of them as necessary for the good of the organization and angrily defend the employer's actions when an outsider questions those actions. In other words, denial of the obvious.[5]

Once, a dear friend of mine repeatedly insisted that she type up a resignation letter on my behalf. She was convinced that I underestimated the gravity of my company's effects on me. To no avail, she attempted to illustrate how I cheapened myself in an unhealthy environment and then persuaded myself to believe that because the company claimed to do good, any misconduct was excusable. She urged me to see how my defense of the company was damaging to my sense of self in ways I couldn't even fathom.

Eyal Winter, Silverzweig Professor of Economics at the Hebrew University of Jerusalem and specialist in behavioral economics, explains that when the balance of power is especially unfavorable for us, our emotional mechanism cooperates with our cognitive mechanism to moderate our feelings of insult and anger. This is rational behavior that in proper measure can reduce potentially damaging friction. In extreme situations, however—for instance, with battered women—that same behavioral pattern can be extremely detrimental. Our emotional mechanism also exaggerates the extent to which we feel gratitude toward figures of authority when they make small and insignificant positive gestures. This can lead us to attach too much importance to such gestures and to develop unsubstantiated trust in the kindness and decency of authority figures.[6]

It's uncomplicated for any woman to believe that her employer, coach, producer, professor, sergeant, elected official, or pastor simply wants the best for her. Her rationale is supported by even the most miniscule of acts—kind words, eye contact, paying for her coffee, nodding supportively to her ideas or proposals in meetings. She is likely not expecting that his compassion and concern will be followed by abuse, rejection, or worse. If she does have a bristling encounter with her superior, she may try to downplay its affects or assume he didn't mean what he said or did, because to her, he's a good man with honorable intentions.

But He's Done So Much for Her

He was the trusted ally, kind and jovial, nerdy and unassuming, unlike the militant gymnastics coaches who tore into girls for the smallest of mistakes. He was the doctor who healed America's top gymnasts who won medals on the world's stage. He was the compassionate soul who was a text or phone call away, on standby for any last-minute emergency. He was the confidant who asked the girls about school, boys, and friends. He was the man who won the trust of parents and a community. He is also the monster who took advantage of innocent girls for more than thirty years.

Many girls who had been sexually abused by Larry Nassar were taken by surprise when initial allegations by the *Indianapolis Star* were made public. The report claimed he molested and fondled young gymnasts.[7] At that point, he was a pillar in the Michigan State University community, an expert doctor for USA Gymnastics, a mainstay at a Junior Olympics gym, and a trusted family friend to hundreds of female athletes and their families.

If parents found themselves strapped for cash after having paid the exorbitant gym fees for their daughter, Nassar would offer to forego billing their insurance for his medical "treatments" to ease the financial burden—*and* to hide any record of his abuse. While young girls, some as young as six, most with no sexual abuse in their past, laid on his massage table, he explained that he could heal their gym injuries, mostly back and hip pain, with invasive treatment. His "treatment," which he performed on over two hundred girls, without gloves or a nurse present, was hardly questioned by parents or authorities because he claimed, in the name of medicine, that it was helpful. Even as girls told him they didn't like it, or that it hurt, he simply responded with, "I know."[8]

After thirty-seven thousand images of child pornography were found by local police on a hard drive in his trash, parents and their daughters wondered if the allegations might be true. What if the goofy doctor who was kind enough to treat girls in his basement after hours, or at a moment's notice, stole from them their innocence? As he honed his predation tactics, Nassar made himself indispensable in the lives of the gymnasts, their families, and other athletes in the Michigan State community. Former USA Gymnastics president Steve Penny "once praised Nassar as being 'instrumental to the success of USA

Gymnastics at many levels, both on and off the field of play.'"[9] Glorified for his hands-on care by many in the profession, Nassar violated the bodies of young girls and left them to deal with their feelings of guilt and shame.

Investigative journalist Abigail Pesta chronicled over a dozen stories in her work *The Girls*, including one volleyball player who vulnerably shared her interior struggle as Nassar sexually assaulted her:

> "I remember laying there wondering, Is this OK? This doesn't seem right," Jennifer Bedford, the former volleyball player, said in her victim impact statement in court, describing how Larry abused her at an appointment while casually chatting away. "There were two arguments at war in my mind: this doesn't seem right, versus, he's a world-renowned doctor who's treated so many athletes," she said. "Everyone knows he treats 'down there,' and they don't complain, so just stop being a baby." Her teammates knew of his unorthodox methods, jokingly calling him the "crotch doc."[10]

Later she shared,

> "In the aftermath, questions raced through my mind a mile a minute, trying to make sense of it all. Could my body really react that way if I didn't want it to? I thought that was impossible," she said in court. "I felt like my body had just betrayed me. I had built up such a wall of protection in my mind around Larry that my first reaction was to question myself, to blame myself. I wanted to believe the best in people, but no matter how much I rationalized—he's a doctor, he's trying to help you, you should be grateful he's treating you, he didn't mean for it to happen—I couldn't shake the voice in my head that said something wasn't right."[11]

Many women who have, in one way or another, been taken advantage of find themselves with an internal dialogue, battling between feeling unsafe and wondering why they would question a person who had the power to keep them safe. They may even claim, "He's done so much for me." If he hasn't advanced the career or path for her, he may have advanced other women's careers, and thus she assumed he could do the same for her. He may even brag about how he's catapulted others to greatness, offering social proof that he is, in fact, more powerful and capable than his prey.

After Harvey Weinstein's predatory behavior and history of sexual assault were exposed in a series of reports in fall of 2017, Gwyneth Paltrow was disgusted to discover that Weinstein would often lure and/or assault women with her name and star-studded track record as bait. He claimed that he could do for them what he did for her, if only they gave in to his unbridled advances. Paltrow commented that "He used the lie as an assault weapon."[12] What these women didn't know was that she herself, at age twenty-two, reported her own sexual harassment by Weinstein to her agent and was expected to remain silent as she continued to work with the award-winning producer who claimed to have made her a household name. No one other than her then-boyfriend, Brad Pitt, a few friends, and her agent knew of the episode. Her silence guaranteed her glamorous roles in successful movies. "She praised Mr. Weinstein publicly, posed for pictures with him and played the glowing star to his powerful producer."[13]

When a woman continues to advance in spaces that fail to report misuses of power, or if she receives special treatment, accolades, and promotions by an untrustworthy, punitive leader without public reprisal, it can lead other women to deduce that the space or leader in question is not the cause of any misfortune or demise but is the path to prominence or, for church folk, righteousness. An added layer to the already deceptive scheme of an abusive leader is when he proclaims to be a person of faith with a functioning moral compass. No one wants to believe a good person is capable of bad things. We are even more willing to turn a blind eye if he has done so much for the church.

Not only do we make excuses for a man who abuses his power, because he has done so much for us, or others in his inner circle. We make excuses because he seemed to selflessly serve the masses. He's the guy who is known for showing up, first on the scene, in the midst of chaos, to help. We couldn't possibly out the kind man who proverbially runs into the burning building when everyone else is running out.

But what if he was the one who set it on fire?

The dichotomous thought process between conscience and career is even more taxing when a man has used his power and resources to advance the greater good, when he adopted fatherless children, raised thousands of dollars for humanitarian causes, gave of his time—morning, noon, and night—with no strings attached, and put himself in harm's way to protect others. Why would we, by telling the truth, betray a man who has advanced society and championed justice? Surely we wouldn't be so foolish. When we stack up his acts of generosity against ours, we fall short of the hero he is.

Betrayal or Truth

For those of us who witness firsthand a victim's trauma, we may first sit in shock and denial, but we later comprehend the truth of the situation. We wrestle with the private knowledge of an offender's actions, complete with sleepless nights and grisly nightmares. We honor the request to keep the experience quiet and not whisper it to a soul, even if we feel as though our world may cave in. At the same time, we fear the ramifications if we were to speak up, upsetting the balance of power and our place within the hierarchy. We may be loyal to the offender and the victim, in which case silence may feel like the safest option, because even though we fear him and fear what would happen to the victim, we fear just as much for his downfall.

In our paralyzed state, we reckon that if we told the truth, we would commit the ultimate betrayal against the offender. Betrayal, in many of our minds, is unforgivable by the betrayed. At least that's what we've gathered from him. More than personal growth or professional achievement, we are certain he values loyalty, and we have seen enough to prove our theory. Maybe we were the ones who had the opportunity to advance and a valued voice at his table. We knew when to keep our mouths zipped and tickle his ears with praise, elaborating on why his opinion on any given issue was the right one. At his invitation, we dismissed and discarded the ideas or projects of others in the name of candor. When someone with a contrarian word spoke up against him, we ensured that we stayed on the preferential side of the offender by disavowing the "pessimist" and his or her naysaying point of view. It was clear that nothing but passionate loyalty was expected and nothing but passionate loyalty was rewarded. Even a whiff of disagreement or betrayal would be snuffed out and handled.

With that awareness, we dodge snitching on him because, as they say, snitches get stitches. While literal stitches will not likely be needed, we imagine the emotional lesions will be devastating. In our minds, we are protecting him *and* us, and consequently we destroy our sense of self and chisel our convictions to dust. Author Dennis S. Reina explains, "Avoiding the truth is a form of betrayal to ourselves and to the people with whom we are in a relationship. By not telling the truth, we compromise our sense of trustworthiness to others and to ourselves."[14] We assume that to betray him is to commit the ultimate sin; in reality, we have betrayed the silenced, the system, and our loyalty to the truth. We believe it is our responsibility to stay silent and protect his name.

PART 2

HOW WE SILENCE WOMEN

My silences had not protected me.
Your silence will not protect you.

—AUDRE LORDE, *YOUR SILENCE
WILL NOT PROTECT YOU*

5

WHAT DO YOU HAVE
TO LOSE?

Why would anyone willingly forfeit their place, stick their own neck out, because of a man's actions? Why would any sane person report a man who brought in millions of dollars, who is seen as a saint by others, and who has more power than they do? Especially if the violation didn't personally happen to them? Bystanders may reckon that, if they have much to lose, then perhaps he has much to gain. When questioned, those who have come forward with accusations claim they aren't trying to retaliate against any sour actions, nor are they keen on being known as the whistleblower who spoke up against a powerful man. They were certain that, once they reported what they knew, those in power would assume they had an ax to grind because the offender had taken away their voice or place. For that reason, bystanders try to carry on and tell themselves that because it didn't happen to them, it is none of their business. That because they don't hold authority over him, it isn't their problem, and because they care for him, they should quietly plot their escape and move on.

How do we silence her? By believing she doesn't need us to break the silence with her, hand in hand. Immediate losses for a silence breaker may seem obvious, but their future opportunities also may be stymied thanks to their truth telling. After silence breakers speak up, the ripple effect of punishment for their disclosure has the potential to rob them of future possibilities. How do silence breakers explain in a future job interview that they are not looking under every rock to expose the misdeeds of the system, but yes, they did report that a former boss/professor/coach/spiritual leader was a pervert who found pleasure in coercing women? If a potential employer called for a reference, what scorching slander would the offender spew to destroy promising prospects?

If bystanders report men who abuse their power, they will likely be benched at work, in their community, in church, or even at home for speaking up against a man others adore, and onlookers may question or misunderstand why they would come forward in the first place. We silence women by assuming that our losses, as bystanders, far outweigh the gains for reporting something that did not happen to us.

Dismayingly, for churchgoers in many faith contexts silence breaking is on par with the work of Satan. I grew up hearing spiritual leaders claim the house of God was under attack by anyone looking to take out God's chosen men who were anointed to lead. Some pastors who see themselves as anointed more than appointed believe that since the burden of leadership is on their shoulders, then Satan would surely be after them and other men charged with caring for the flock. While I do not disagree with the idea that pastors are under enormous pressure, the idea that attacks against them are direct attacks against the gospel are a stretch when a perceived "attack" is a truthful account of their own misconduct. Add to this the misconception that attacks on the church and its leaders must mean the church and its leaders are making an impact for the kingdom and thus have become targets for those who do not want to see them succeed. I'm confident that no woman who has been harmed by a "godly" man and then bravely speaks up wants herself or her allies to be called enemies of the gospel.

A woman's dissent against the actions of a "chosen" leader can backfire so quickly that she hardly has time to prepare for her baptism by firing squad, and witnesses who could stand up for her flee the scene for fear of guilt by association. Femme fatale, a tool of the devil, a distraction from kingdom work, a jezebel looking to take out God's anointed man—these colorful labels are only a sampling of the church lexicon reserved for women who break the silence and speak up against avowedly God-fearing men, or any wolf in shepherd's clothing.

In faith communities, those with a story to report concerning a church leader that will inevitably paint the Christian ecclesia in a poor light are often warned not to harm the church at large or speak ill of the Lord's anointed—a conduit of higher power. Taken out of context and weaponized against whistle-blowers, David's warning to his men, and to himself, not to touch the Lord's anointed (1 Sam. 24:10) is misused by clergy, board members, and churchgoers alike when it provides an air of untouchability and silence where accountability and truth telling are wholeheartedly necessary.

In 1 Samuel, David is publicly at odds with Saul's choices as anointed leader of the Israelites but does not physically harm him. When presented with the opportunity of a sleeping, vulnerable Saul in a cave, David does not murder his someday-predecessor's life in hopes of ending his own troubles. How that moment in biblical history has translated to power-hungry pastors that shirk culpability is disheartening to say the least.

Let us not forget that later, in 2 Samuel 11, King David sends his royal aides to bring Bathsheba to him after he has invaded her privacy by voyeuristically watching her bathe herself after her "monthly uncleanliness" from his palace rooftop. Abusing every ounce of his God-given power, he rapes Bathsheba, an innocent woman and wife to another man. Bathsheba finds her body, mind, and soul devoured by David's thirsty appetite. She is not a vixen who seduces him, but a victim of sexual assault. Diana R. Garland, dean of social work at Baylor University, notes, "Bathsheba was a victim of a man with authority, the leader of his people, abusing his power—something akin to employer sexual harassment or clergy sexual abuse today."[1] David clearly exploits the power imbalance between himself and Bathsheba.

As the story goes, once King David receives word that Bathsheba is pregnant, he commands Uriah the Hittite, Bathsheba's husband, to take a leave of absence in hopes that Uriah will lie with his wife and mask David's consequences. When Uriah does not act as David has hoped, David effectively commits murder by insisting Uriah fight on the front lines. The prophet Nathan confronts David with a story about a man who took advantage of his place and power to steal from the vulnerable. Enraged by the story, David discovers that he is the man who has capitalized on his power, and by God's grace, Nathan's bold confrontation ultimately leads to David's sincere repentance. The God of Israel forgives David, but consequences are still dealt to the guilty king by way of death and destruction.

Second Samuel 12:9–12 outlines a lifetime of consequences for King David:

> "Why did you despise the word of the Lord by doing what is evil in his eyes? You struck down Uriah the Hittite with the sword and took his wife to be your own. You killed him with the sword of the Ammonites. Now, therefore, the sword will never depart from your house, because you despised me and took the wife of Uriah the Hittite to be your own."
>
> This is what the Lord says: "Out of your own household I am going to bring calamity on you. Before your very eyes I will take

your wives and give them to one who is close to you, and he will sleep with your wives in broad daylight. You did it in secret, but I will do this thing in broad daylight before all Israel."

The son born to Bathsheba dies because of David's utter contempt for the Lord (2 Sam. 12:14). Later, his own son Amnon will rape his daughter Tamar, and her brother Absalom will go on to battle him for the seat of king. David is disgraced by those beneath him, he later faces revolt by another one of his offspring, and he has only a slice of the favor he had before he took advantage of his limitless power. David has been caught, and even the Alpha and the Omega isn't about to bury the hatchet without retribution. David faces dire consequences for his actions, yet stone-in-the-slingshot David, known by his famous moniker "the man after the Lord's own heart" (see 1 Sam. 13:14), is routinely paraded in contemporary Christian circles as an example of how sinful a man is, yet God can, and will, still use him. It doesn't matter if he is a president, preacher, or pastor. Why? Because he's chosen, but let's not forget that David, with a heart of humility, repented for what he stole from Bathsheba as the prophet Nathan spoke up to illustrate his sin and how it grieved the heart of Father God.

Rather than call for leaders to recognize and repent of their misconduct, I've heard men and women take the stage to pray that no weapon formed against their male headship would prosper and every tongue that rose against them in judgment would be condemned. They professed that this was their leaders' inheritance in the Lord (Isa. 54:17). In ecclesiastical contexts where abuse of power is reported, this verse is misapplied, along with others, to those charged with caring for the flock. I am wholeheartedly committed to praying for my church leaders, yet "a weapon formed against them" should never be the label we slap on claims of misconduct.

In many cases, if pastors are accused of egregious actions, they remind parishioners to turn the other cheek when attacked (Matt. 5:39) as *they* humbly demonstrate—although foes have attacked the pastors, they will respond in love and pray for those who persecuted them (Matt. 5:44). Nothing makes a manipulative pastor look better than claiming the moral high ground and forgiving the accused for their bravery while never taking responsibility for their own actions. Whether in the face of false accusations or legitimate accusations, this "godly" response seems to fit the bill. It's not uncommon to witness ministry leaders use these sanctimonious tactics when accused of misconduct, even quoting Jesus's words in Luke 23:34 toward their accusers: "Father, forgive them, for they know not what they do" (ESV).

The last thing any person wants is for their church community to believe they vilified an abusive man for personal gain, weren't thankful for his mentorship, or that they are against, in some bizarre way, the advancement of the kingdom, when in reality, they deeply love the church. Such was the case when good men and women spoke out against a Midwest pastor with an outsized influence who labeled his accusers as "colluders" seeking to discredit his ministry with lies. Despite testimonies from credible witnesses that spanned several decades, the pastor maintained his position of innocence against the accusations and placed the spotlight on those looking to vilify his leadership.[2] As much as we'd love to believe that the church might handle misconduct differently than mainstream culture, there is no wrath quite like the wrath of holy men caught in the transgressions they condemn.

We Forgive Men but Not Women

I was twelve when I first glanced at a photo of a young, blushing brunette with a beret atop her head and maroon lipstick shining from her lips. She donned the cover of nearly every magazine at the grocery store checkout. The smiling woman, previously unknown to the public, would sadly become a household name for reasons that still make us blush. Traditional and freshly developed online media reported to the American people that their saxophone-playing president, at age forty-nine, had alleged sexual relations with a twenty-two-year-old White House intern.

Second-term president Bill Clinton was scorned for his inappropriate actions with Monica Lewinsky and faced impeachment by the House of Representatives after it was discovered that he had lied about the relationship before a grand jury and attempted to obstruct the investigation into his misbehavior. He was caught with enough evidence to prove what he had done and faced public shame.

The majority of Americans chose to overlook the president's private wrongdoing because his public impact, in their minds, superseded the act he committed and proved to be unrelated to his role as the leader of the free world. While Clinton's approval ratings dipped for a short time, he bounced back to a higher approval rating than he had *before* the affair was made known to the press and the people. Gallup notes that Clinton's sexual predation and lying under oath occurred at a time when "the American public was unusually positive in its ratings of the economy and of its overall satisfaction with the way things were going in the country."[3]

Clinton led during a time of economic growth, and in return, the public forgave his misconduct by way of higher-than-expected approval ratings—in fact, he left office with the highest rating of any predecessor in fifty years.[4] He no doubt lost respectability as he was impeached by the House of Representatives, but Clinton later was and still is largely respected by the public as he speaks around the world, is interviewed by esteemed publications on his leadership style, and campaigns for the Democratic Party.

While Clinton received forgiveness and a continued place in the public eye, Monica Lewinsky was painted on the American landscape as a whore.

Writing for *Vanity Fair* in 2014, Lewinsky professed, "Sure, my boss took advantage of me, but I will always remain firm on this point: it was a consensual relationship. Any 'abuse' came in the aftermath, when I was made a scapegoat in order to protect his powerful position. . . . The Clinton administration, the special prosecutor's minions, the political operatives on both sides of the aisle, and the media were able to brand me. And that brand stuck, in part because it was imbued with power."[5]

Lewinsky, in her early twenties, withstood blunt-force hits, one after another, by the media, the power players who protected the Clinton administration, and even rappers. (No joke, at the time of this writing, Lewinsky's name has made the cut in 128 rap songs.[6]) She was the scapegoat for a forty-nine-year-old's actions behind closed doors, and no one was going to let the world forget it, not even Beyoncé.

Despite the fact that Clinton had faced numerous sexual harassment allegations and, in the case of Juanita Brodderick, an allegation of rape, Clinton was the one the public forgave while Lewinsky faced public scorn. In a public apology, he shared, "What I want the American people to know, what I want the Congress to know is that I am profoundly sorry for all I have done wrong in words and deeds. I never should have misled the country, the Congress, my friends or my family. Quite simply, I gave in to my shame."[7] Between Clinton's apology, expert damage control from high-profile publicists, and the silence of Lewinsky, the media pegged Lewinsky as the home wrecker, the flirt, and the reason for Clinton's downfall.

Lewinsky continued to suffer for her actions as Clinton maintained his place of power in the public eye. Her mother worried she might take her life due to the relentless humiliation; landing a job unrelated to her high-profile scandal was nearly impossible.[8]

Two decades before the #MeToo and #ChurchToo movements pushed to amplify the voices of women who have been sexually harassed, assaulted, or otherwise demeaned, Lewinsky experienced a manipulation of the narrative in which the blame was shifted onto her. Like Lewinsky, ordinary women have faced the same exasperating contempt in varying degrees in their workplaces and churches. While no one is perfect, it's striking that men are forgiven for their misbehavior even while women continue to suffer. In many cases, if even a whiff of unforgiveness is detected after a woman discloses misconduct, she is routinely asked by pastors and spiritual leaders, "But have you forgiven him?"

In faith settings, a bent toward forgiving male perpetrators is so heavily emphasized, often early in the process of healing, that victims of misconduct, and those who've been indirectly affected by the perpetrator, are presumed to be vindictive or immature if they do not swiftly forgive their perpetrators. For the sake of their own soul, they are told, they must forgive those who have harmed them or they forfeit right standing with God. (You know, small stuff.) Matthew 6:14–15 says, "For if you forgive other people when they sin against you, your heavenly Father will also forgive you. But if you do not forgive others their sins, your Father will not forgive your sins."

Without question, forgiveness is key to healing. As victims pursue healing of their mind, body, and soul after sexual misconduct, forgiveness of the perpetrator is part of the process. However, when the gravity of the harm is not taken into full consideration, and compassion and care for the victim are seen as secondary to the victim's offer of forgiveness, it downplays the significant impact perpetrators have, reducing the victims' experiences to trivial encounters. We can best serve women who have been silenced by encouraging them to heal, but never by instructing them to heal by immediately forgiving their perpetrators. Forgiveness is necessary, but not on a predetermined timeline we've created for those who've been harmed that slyly makes us feel better about the situation and paints the perpetrator in flattering colors.

Even more damaging is the urging of forgiveness for the sake of reconciliation with the perpetrator despite apparent harm and distress. Women, no matter who they are, where they've come from, or what they've experienced, deserve physical, emotional, and spiritual safety, and the encouragement of parishioners to pursue reconciliation at all costs easily places harmed women back in harm's way. People of faith urging reconciliation before the perpetrator is held responsible for harming others can lead victims to be further coerced and abused.

When wives are instructed by ministry leaders or girlfriends from Bible study to return to their abusive husband and "love him to health," or parishioners are told to endure emotional abuse, Scripture verses inviting us to love, forgive, and reconcile with others are misappropriated. These include Colossians 3:13, "Bear with each other and forgive one another if any of you has a grievance against someone. Forgive as the Lord forgave you"; or Ephesians 4:32, "Be kind and compassionate to one another, forgiving each other, just as in Christ God forgave you"; or Hebrews 12:14, "Make every effort to live in peace with everyone and to be holy; without holiness no one will see the Lord." Forgiveness, according to Luke 17:3, is in response to repentance, and a rebuke is necessary in response to sin. Persuading women to be ambassadors of forgiveness and reconciliation in unsafe environments teaches women that their safety and well-being are of no concern when men abuse their power to harm them. Reconciliation should be reserved for repentant individuals, not perpetrators who have no interest in turning from their ways. Honesty and truth must precede reconciliation.

For years, I've heard from pillars of the faith that reconciliation is one of our primary objectives as followers of Jesus. With that as a central value to the Christian faith, I felt as though my refusal to reconcile with those who've abused their power would be a mark against my maturity rather than a necessary boundary in place to protect myself.

Not only are we encouraged to forgive men when they harm women; in many instances, women are inordinately punished for the same infractions men commit. In one study from three scholars from Harvard, Stanford, and the University of Texas, evidence of a "gender punishment gap" found that women in the financial industry were 20 percent more likely to lose their jobs and face harsher consequences relative to male colleagues for the same misconduct.[9] Betty Dukes explained that same sentiment in her statement before the Senate Judiciary Committee when she sued her employer, Walmart, arguing that she suffered "from discipline for actions which men were free to take without punishment."[10] Sadly, consequences that exist in theory for men are regularly enforced on women, no matter if they are a young White House intern, seasoned financial adviser, or reliable Walmart greeter. *Time* notes, "In today's workplaces, we cannot assume that employees will be equally hit with the same punishment for the same misdeeds. This form of discrimination affects women and minorities in pay raises and dismissals."[11] No matter where a woman works, the likelihood that she will be punished in ways that her male counterparts won't for the same incidents, or even minor incidents, leaves her with more to lose and even less to gain in trying to right wrongs.

Whistleblowers

No one likes a tattletale—not the little girl who overheard plans to bully the kid with braces on the playground and told the person on recess duty, or the woman who relays to human resources specifics of her superior's nefarious deeds. Such a woman may be seen as punching above her pay grade, too willing to sacrifice the trust of her colleagues, and abandoning herd values. Her institution may push for honesty and transparency so as long as those in power remain there. If her honesty and transparency expose iniquities that jeopardize the institution, then tattletale beware.

Whistleblowers, those who publicize alleged illegal or unethical behavior, are sometimes seen as sellouts, out to make a buck as they squawk about the crooked conditions or mishaps by the institution's shot callers. At other times, they are seen as brave reporters who speak up for the good of the institution. It all depends on who is telling the story. Pulitzer Prize–winning journalists Frederik Obermaier and Bastian Obermayer claim that "whisleblowers . . . are regarded as vital to open societies, but there are few laws to effectively protect them. When they're revealed along with the secrets they uncover, they often end up marginalized, shamed or, worse, threatened. People love the betrayal, but not the betrayer."[12]

Despite laws in all fifty states protecting whistleblowers to some degree, those who accuse their superiors of wrongdoing face collateral damage. Once the proverbial cat is out of the bag, the consequential reaction is to slice and dice the whistleblower's character, motivations, and track record. Instead of the spotlight being placed squarely on the purported misconduct, the bright lights burn on the face of the accuser. The one who is accused claims betrayal at the hands of an angry woman, an aid of the Enemy, and the accuser is attacked by the regime appointed to lead a smear campaign in hopes of destroying her credibility.

Whistleblowers, regardless of context, often face reprisal—intimidation, threats, demotions, gossip, slander—and if they speak up against their employer, there is potential job loss for supposed unrelated reasons. Such was the case for Melissa Lonner after she reported to superiors that the host of *Today*, Matt Lauer, sexually propositioned her. Executives encouraged Lonner to stay on board despite her claims, and she did. After her contract expired, it was not renewed by NBC. Only later did she learn that her "delayed departure prevented her from raising harassment claims due to their statutes of limitations." Upon her exit, her agent brokered routine nondisclosure and nondisparagement clauses, which included a six-figure payout in exchange for signing a release of rights.[13] In the end, Lonner was jobless, silenced, and unable to defend herself against any slander NBC or Lauer might spew to sully her reputation. Sharing her traumatizing experience ultimately led to her professional demise. Roomy Khan, an expert on white-collar crimes, rightly notes, "Society celebrates team players and snubs naysayers, and therein lies the stigma—'snitch or rat.'"[14]

Our primal need to belong—in the office, neighborhood, gym, church, and so on—clashes with our internal compass when we experience or witness misconduct. If we choose to stay within a broken system and remain silent about our experiences, we may continue to feel accepted, yet belonging within a vicious system that values silence over safety, or routinely defrocks silence breakers, hinders not only the whistleblower or victims but everyone subject to the system.

6

THE QUESTIONING

"Why did you wait to speak up?"
"Why didn't you call the police?"
"What were you wearing?"
"Why didn't you flee the scene?"
"Why didn't you fight back?"
"Why didn't you close your legs?"
"Did you ask for it?"
"Did you lead him on?"

These questions, posed by judges, lawyers, board members, human resource personnel, pastors, and friends assume that the victim somehow did not employ her agency to fight off her offender. Underneath their questions lie beliefs about what they deem as an appropriate response to sexual misconduct, as well as judgment for the victim. They may assume the victim, with her sultry eyes and tight-fitted clothes, invited misconduct. The offender may admit he engaged the victim but blames her because he couldn't help himself when she clearly asked for it—not with words, mind you, but with the unspoken rules of enticement.

The proverbial and literal judge and jury ask: If she didn't want sexual attention, then why did she dress like that? Why did she carry herself the way she did? Why did she laugh at his jokes? Why was she so gracious and kind with him? Surely it means she was into him. Didn't she put herself in a position to be preyed upon, anyway? Didn't she realize what would happen at late-night meetings, on business trips, with the promise of promotions? Didn't she know that if she let a man like that in her world, he'll do what men are born to do? Doesn't she know what happens to women after dark?

One judge in New Jersey, John F. Russo Jr., questioned a woman seeking a restraining order against a man who sexually assaulted her, threatened her life, and made inappropriate comments about her child. When insensitively asked by Judge Russo if she knew how to fend off intercourse, the woman replied that she would physically fight her attacker and run away. Unsatisfied with her answer, Russo rebuffed her response with his own answers in the form of questions: "Block your body parts? Close your legs? Call the police?" Since she was an exotic dancer, Russo claimed, she should have known how to protect herself from unwanted advances. The woman, who expressed imminent danger, left the court without a restraining order against her assailant. When questioned about his behavior from the bench, Russo claimed he helped a demoralized witness express herself.[1]

Just to the north, in New York State, another victim's answers to legal questioning inadvertently aided in reduced sentences for her rapists. In the fall of 2017, at eighteen years old, Anna Chambers was pulled over, cuffed, and thrown into the back of a van by plainclothes detectives while her friends, both males, were free to go after they were caught with marijuana. The Brooklyn South narcotics unit detectives, Eddie Martins and Richard Hall, reportedly forced Chambers to remove her bra in their search for alleged drugs, told her friends not to follow the van, and then drove around and took turns forcibly raping her in the backseat while she lay handcuffed, begging them to stop. About an hour later, Chambers was dropped by the side of the road, not far from where she was first arrested. Traumatized as she walked along the street, Chambers asked to borrow a stranger's phone to call a friend. A few hours later at the hospital with her mother, Chambers reported that she had been raped by two police officers. Semen from her rape kit matched the DNA of both officers and traffic cams caught the officers dropping her off, just a stone's throw from a police precinct.[2] Chambers expected both officers to be charged for rape, but no such charges were made. Why? Her answers to defense lawyers' biased questions coupled with a loophole maintaining it's not illegal for police officers to have sex with someone in their custody. While sexual contact by probation officers and prison and jail guards is outlawed, police officers in several states are not subject to what should be a commonsense law.

Chambers' rapists resigned from their positions after they were indicted but kept to a story claiming that Chambers was a temptress, therefore they had not broken the law. When hammered by the detectives' defense attorneys with questions about the evening, Chambers reported that the sex acts were not consensual as evidenced by the unmistakable imbalance of power. When asked what she wore on the evening of the assault, Chambers claimed she wore a skirt, while in reality she wore track pants. She claimed she noticed identifiable landmarks outside the van window, but cell data didn't confirm the route that would have included the named landmarks (which I can only imagine would have been difficult to remember while being assaulted by not one man, but two, twice her size). Despite DNA evidence that she was assaulted, because she could not, as an eighteen-year-old girl, expound on specific details, and due to social media posts like that of her in a bikini, making dirty jokes, or confessing she went to a porn convention, rape charges were dropped citing "unforeseen and serious credibility issues." Rather than a prison sentence, Chambers' rapists received five years of probation.[3] Not exactly what you would expect for two men who abused their power—or perhaps it is, after questioning "the lesser sex."

Chambers' confused testimony, experts note, is not unheard of when a victim is asked to recall traumatic events. Trauma specialist and psychologist Dr. Hillary McBride explains why this can happen:

> When we experience trauma, our brain and nervous system changes how we store memory. What would otherwise be a clear, coherent story about an experience characterized by safety or normalcy can become a choppy or disorganized narrative. Because of the change in how memory is encoded during these traumatic moments . . . some elements feel exaggerated and looming, while other details seem irrelevant, shrink to the background of our awareness, or seem to never have been stored at all. What this means is that when victims and survivors of trauma are asked to tell their stories, to family members, police, investigators, or on the stand as a witness in a trial, is that the story of the trauma can appear jumbled or unclear, the recounting of the details may even change based on the person's physiological state while answering questions or [depending on] who is asking the questions. While this has been used to discredit survivors, women who've lived through sexual abuse, assault, and violence, it is often proof of the trauma itself. [4]

In addition, sexual misconduct laws and rulings reveal bias within the justice system that discriminate against women and uphold rape culture. The Women's Center at Marshall University defines rape culture as "an environment in which rape is prevalent and in which sexual violence against women is normalized and excused in the media and popular culture. Rape culture is perpetuated through the use of misogynistic language, the objectification of women's bodies, and the glamorization of sexual violence, thereby creating a society that disregards women's rights and safety."[5] The accepted norms—influenced by rape culture, church culture, and determined within court systems—trickle down to the places we work and worship. It leads management and ministers to ask questions that:

- trivialize harassment and assault
- assume a level of tolerance for sexually explicit joking
- assume a level of tolerance for sexual harassment
- scrutinize a woman's appearance
- define men as dominant
- define women as submissive
- pressure women to put up with abusive men in authority
- presume women are promiscuous
- assume men deserve sex and sexual stimulation
- presume women of color are hypersexual
- assign intent or motive to women

Questions laced with assumptions that are asked by high courts and holy men have long perpetuated harmful gender stereotypes. During the time of chattel slavery endured by African Americans, Black women were subject to sexual coercion without any legal protection from the law. However, in 1874 a fourteen-year-old servant's case was heard before New York's High Court. She was forcibly raped by her employer after he locked her in his barn and sent away her younger siblings. In response to her case, the question was asked, "Can the mind conceive of a woman, in the possession of her faculties and powers, revoltingly unwilling that this deed should be done upon her, who would not resist so hard and so long as she was able? And if a woman, aware that it will be done unless she does resist, does not resist to the extent of her ability on the occasion, must it not be that she is not entirely reluctant? If consent, though not express, enters into her conduct, there is no rape."[6]

At that time, and in many ways now, "the law assumed that women in fact *wanted* the sexual advances and assaults that they claimed injured them," notes Reva Siegel, professor of law at Yale Law School. She adds,

> Unless women could show that they had performed an elaborate ritual of resistance, perfect compliance with the legally specified terms of which was necessary to overcome the overwhelming presumption that women latently desired whatever was sexually done to them, they could expect little recourse from the criminal law. Rape law's protection was further vitiated by the fact that prosecutors and judges relied on all kinds of race- and class-based assumptions about the "promiscuous" natures of the women in domestic service and other forms of market labor as they reasoned about utmost resistance.[7]

For heaven's sake, no woman *invites* sexual violation because of her skin pigment, class status, immigration status, or religion. Yet those sexist theories continue to thread themselves through questions aimed at victimized women to this present day.

We might assume that women with power would be treated differently, but it's not always the case, according to research reported in the *American Sociological Review*. "Having power and authority does not protect women from harassment, it actually increases its likelihood. Powerful women pose a threat to men's position in the gender hierarchy, which motivates them to undermine those women and their authority through sexual harassment."[8] Class-based and, arguably, raced-based stereotypes fall short, if even women with power are harassed and assaulted.

When assumptions bias the questioning of victims, it does not provide room to listen and learn. It simply assigns blame—robbing a victim of her story, her unique trauma that we have no business assuming we understand. We weren't there. We didn't feel her fear. Addressing the bias of blame within dominant culture and the Christian tradition requires a revisionist imagination, as both have historically blamed women for their harm.

At one point, early in my career, a superior locked eyes with me and said, "My God, you're beautiful." He then took the time to compliment my aptitude and assets, only after he praised my physical appearance. Just your everyday, run-of-the-mill, professional praise intermixed with harassment. After my "compliments," I felt as though that was just the way the world works. If I didn't want him to comment, I reasoned in my young mind, maybe *I* should do something different. Since he wasn't going to change, I presumed it on was on me to change the outcome, because he couldn't help but let the lust of the flesh consume him.

As a follower of Jesus who came of age during the 1990s purity movement, which sought to popularize abstinence with promise rings, pledges, and purity balls amid what evangelicals believed was a lascivious era, I internalized the belief that I, with my female gaze, growing chest, and hip-hugger jeans, could cause my brother to stumble if I wasn't careful. Men were visual creatures, I was told, and therefore it was up to me and my sisters in the Lord to ensure our brothers didn't stumble due to our appearance. White T-shirts, spaghetti straps, and cleavage-bearing swimsuits were clearly off limits because they would undoubtedly attract unwanted male attention. Men were burdened with ravenous lust, but my fellow sisters in Christ and I had the wherewithal to set boundaries because we weren't bound by the same primal desires as men. Plus, I was warned, my body belonged to my future husband, and even an imprudent thought, let alone sexual immorality in my teen years, would sabotage any chance for a fulfilling marriage.

While my marriage has been a treasured gift, these messages that I was responsible for how males perceived me did foster enmity between my mind and body, and it took years to reconcile that my body, mind, and spirit are interconnected. My body, it turns out, wasn't dirty and capable of making boys stumble, and it took years to believe that was true.

Lest you think my youth was lacking in good counsel, I did receive appreciable advice on values to search for in a potential mate; encouragement to hold my heart, mind, and body in high regard; an understanding of why faithfulness in an intimate relationship fosters wholeness and connection; and a broad grasp on how porn erodes the ability to connect. However, the notion that I retained control over men's downfall was harmful and led to feelings of shame for simply living in a woman's body. I held to this belief throughout my twenties, and it ultimately contributed to my silence in the broken systems I found myself in.

To right the cultural wrong of shaming women's bodies, we must overhaul how we think about women's bodies as something to be used or abused and put a full stop to victim blaming. The presumption that women are to be damsels in distress (purity culture) or to be dominated (rape culture) paints women as prey, not as equals with agency to determine what happens to their bodies or lives. Interestingly, purity culture and rape culture have always had one notion in common: that a woman's body is not her own but belongs to a man. Both cultures equate respectability with safety and assume women are culpable if defiled, because in order to be violated, they must have strayed from patriarchal standards ensuring their protection. However, a woman is not to be stripped of agency, consent, or boundaries because another deems her unworthy of such standards, and it is wholly destructive to believe that what happens to her body is her fault when she has no choice in the matter.

The worst is when a victim feels as though unwanted advances are her fault. Blame from the offender, criminal justice system, her superiors, mainstream culture, the church, and her own mind only bury the truth that she is a victim in need of compassionate care rather than someone deserving harassment or assault. Believing that the victim suffers from low self-esteem and purposely seeks out emotional, physical, or sexual harm only halts the societal sympathy needed to overcome the resulting trauma. In addition, it preserves the lie that a woman, by her very nature, is responsible for actions perpetrated against her. Until she learns it wasn't her fault, she stalls telling her story.

Why Women Wait to Tell the Truth

It's not uncommon for a considerable amount of time to pass before a woman, or someone with firsthand knowledge of misconduct, comes forward and reports what happened at the hands of a dominant and powerful man. Any woman who has endured or witnessed something in private is not necessarily eager to discuss her claims in public, but eventually the weight of it all is too much to carry. To lay it down means to speak up about the experience and admit the havoc it's wreaked on her life.

Shaila Dewan, writing for the *New York Times*, notes, "Negative consequences are not the only thing to keep victims from coming forward. Experts point to a more fundamental issue: When the perpetrator is someone they trusted, it can take years for victims even to identify what happened to them as a violation."[9]

Reah Bravo is one of several women who reported that the broadcast journalist Charlie Rose made unwanted sexual advances to her. The *Washington Post* reported that for Bravo, "it has taken 10 years and a fierce moment of cultural reckoning for me to understand these moments for what they were."[10] Fear of retaliation, feelings of guilt and shame, and a desire to move on without the impending stress sure to accompany a public claim is enough to keep many women from speaking up for a long time. For many women, years after their experiences, they struggle to grasp that what happened *actually* happened.

In her book *Know My Name*, Chanel Miller, sexual assault survivor of Stanford University student Brock Turner, speaks to why it can take considerable time for assault victims to come forward. She writes,

> Some called it a witch hunt, said she's after him. I ask, starting when. Mark the day. Trace it back. I can almost guarantee that after the assault she tried to live her life. Ask her what she did the next day and she'd say, well, I went to work. She didn't pick up a pitchfork, hire a lawyer. She made her bed, buttoned up her shirt, took shower after shower. She tried to believe she was unchanged, to move on until her legs gave out. Every woman who spoke out did so because she hit a point where she could no longer live another day in the life she tried to build. So she turned, slowly, back around to face it. Society thinks we live to come after him. When in fact, we live to live. That's it. He's upended that life, and we tried to keep going but we couldn't. Each time a survivor resurfaced, people were quick to say what does she want, why did it take her so long, why now, why not then, why not faster. But damage does not stick to deadlines. If she emerges, why don't we ask her how it was possible she lived with that hurt for so long, ask who taught her to never uncover it?[11]

I'm not sure there is anything quite as tragic as asking a woman who is brave enough to speak truth to power and tell the unsavory details of her story or what she has witnessed why she waited so long to come forward if the claims she reports are really that deplorable. Why didn't she immediately report what she knew? Instead of placing oneself in her shoes, those in power judge why she didn't come forward, why she stayed in proximity to *him*. Why she didn't "act" like someone who had been harassed or harmed. For those who report on behalf of others, the questions are similar. Why didn't she narc on her friend or colleague earlier? Why did she continue to work for him if it was really that sour of a work environment? If she knew, what was she hoping to gain by staying that long? Or my personal favorite, for the whistleblowers in a Christian context: Why didn't she go to him directly and work it out, Matthew 18 style?

The Misuse of Matthew 18

Matthew 18:15–20 states,

> If your brother or sister sins, go and point out their fault, just between the two of you. If they listen to you, you have won them over. But if they will not listen, take one or two others along, so that "every matter may be established by the testimony of two or three witnesses." If they still refuse to listen, tell it to the church; and if they refuse to listen even to the church, treat them as you would a pagan or a tax collector.
>
> Truly I tell you, whatever you bind on earth will be bound in heaven, and whatever you loose on earth will be loosed in heaven.
>
> Again, truly I tell you that if two of you on earth agree about anything they ask for, it will be done for them by my Father in heaven. For where two or three gather in my name, there am I with them.

I can see what well-meaning folks are hinting at. Why would anyone need go over their pastor's head and bring a governing board into the picture? Have they not read the good book? Go to your brother, it says. If someone with accusations does not follow that clear principle, they must be a pot stirrer, out to ruin the ministry of a man who has only ever served spiritually starved souls.

In some manipulative situations, according to those elected to oversee spiritual leaders, silence breakers aren't familiar with how things of this nature should be handled, and their hope of reporting the truth is misguided. Even worse is when overseers are coached by the offender, who is doing damage control, grasping at whatever he can to protect himself from accusations that hold weight. As silence breakers attempt to shed light on dark deeds, the Matthew 18 argument is played like a trump card, and it leaves brave souls feeling incredibly guilty for not confronting their spiritual leader directly.

In some cases, silence breakers fail to verbalize their thought process when asked why they didn't directly address their "brother" in the Lord. What they neglect to admit is that they fear becoming a victim of slander or retribution by the spiritual leader, perhaps not nearly to the degree as those he took advantage of, but a fear rooted in reality since they've seen him use his power against those he despises. Instead of sharing their point of view that they hoped, in retrospect, would have caused overseers to soften, they are questioned and shamed for mishandling the sensitive information. Silence breakers didn't handle it biblically, they are told.

The instructions found in Matthew 18 make their way into faith-based staff manuals and are often quoted during employee meetings as a way to handle inner-office conflict. Rather than report the issue to human resources, employees are instructed to first "Matthew 18" it over issues that arise. While I do believe that Matthew 18 is clear on approaching a brother or sister in the Lord when there is dissension between them, this might work for horizonal relationships but it gets murky in the world of vertical leadership. Those working for a narcissistic leader are keenly aware of how their boss may operate when backed into a corner. Yet when an issue arises that a silence breaker can no longer ignore, their boss becomes their "brother" and not their spiritual leader, or employer (per Matt. 18:15). Spiritual leaders don't often make a habit of admitting to anything dirty or dishonest, so when overseers encourage silence breakers to approach the man who employs them—the one who claims to be their compassionate leader—and share with him their grievances, this equates to asking them to willingly walk off a plank.

If those with credible accusations did not first approach the leader but instead reached above his head, they may be warned not to sully a good man's name. But many with the guts to speak up hope going to the leader's superiors will lead to some sort of protection. They hope to be cared for and consoled for how their leader has emotionally, spiritually, mentally, or sexually taken advantage of his position. Many silence breakers who speak up on behalf of the victimized are told that since the information is secondhand—since they personally didn't experience violation—they cannot address the situation unless others come forward, but as a result of approaching superiors, the hope of an offender controlling the narrative is spoiled. Remorseful as a silence breaker likely already feels for approaching leadership, there is victory for speaking up and saying out loud what rings like an alarm between one's ears.

Overseers who claim that silence breakers have not followed proper procedure according to Matthew 18 are scripturally naive and misguided. Requesting that a parishioner or employee approach his or her spiritual leader on matters of misconduct is ill-advised. The sins reported are against oneself and another and, as 1 Timothy instructs, are to be reported to the elders as they stand in authority over the spiritual leader. Here is the text of 1 Timothy 5:19–20: "Do not admit a charge against an elder except on the evidence of two or three witnesses. As for those who persist in sin, rebuke them in the presence of all, so that the rest may stand in fear" (ESV).

The instruction of 1 Timothy 5 does not ask for accusations to be brought to the spiritual leader before approaching elders. It is the responsibility of the elders to pursue witnesses and settle the matter *justly* and, if holding Romans 13:1–2 in high regard, *legally* as well. Matthew 18:15–20 and 1 Timothy 5:19–20 do not provide contradictory directives but address contrasting issues in distinct relationships. Matthew 18:15–20 instructs believers in relationships with brothers and sisters in the family of God, and 1 Timothy 5:19–20 instructs believers in relationships with spiritual headship.[12]

In faith contexts or not, nothing singes the skin like being told your bravery was mismanaged. That your commitment to do what was right was out of line. It's doubtful that overseers, in that moment, understand that by interrogating a silence breaker with insensitive questions when that person comes forward makes for subtle slander—vilifying the experience and testimony, all in an effort to protect a predator. Yet, as we speak up, we can dismantle, abolish, and crush the patriarchy.

7

PUPPETS OF THE PATRIARCHY

An offender often has accomplices—men and women who will do anything for him. They will excuse his behavior and drop everything to meet his whims. If they've made it into his inner circle and serve as gatekeepers to those on the outside, then they are likely the ones to do his bidding. They have proximity to power, privilege dependent on his position, and they enable his abusive behavior with their undying support and willingness to execute his plans. Anyone who has influence and whom he can influence has a chance for a spot on the inside.

His loyal puppets wear an invisible badge of honor as they scurry about and whisper to him in hushed tones, making it their goal to keep him happy. They may be the ones to stride into an office, house, Bible study, or meeting with a message to deliver that he doesn't care to deliver himself. They ensure things are done his way. It doesn't matter if they exhibit high-caliber character; it matters only that he can trust them.

His loyal supporters would hardly describe themselves as puppets manipulated by a puppet master, but their actions speak volumes—like the faithful assistant who never misses a beat in executing his orders, no matter how bizarre or suspect, or the second-in-command who sits in silence while he berates others in his presence. Others show their support by what they don't say. Their endorsement is hidden in their knowing glances and smirks, little eye rolls and muffled laughs. He says too much, and they say nothing, and by not saying anything, they validate his behavior.

Growing up, I learned that those in the faith community operate not in a democracy but rather in the "culture of the kingdom," which meant I was to honor the monarch at all costs. Hebrews 13:17 was internalized to mean that I was obligated to obey my leaders, no matter the sacrifice they demanded. The verse says, "Have confidence in your leaders and submit to their authority, because they keep watch over you as those who must give an account. Do this so that their work will be a joy, not a burden, for that would be of no benefit to you."

Hebrews 13:17 does not, much to the chagrin of abusive leaders everywhere, demand blind loyalty. Ten verses before, Hebrews 13:7 instructs believers to consider the outcome of their leaders' way of life and imitate their faith. In Hebrews 13:9, believers are warned not to be carried away by strange teachings. An overall encouragement to be critically minded concerning leaders in Hebrews 13 invites believers to question and assess authoritarian leadership styles rather than submit to them.

Too many women are told to unflinchingly bow to a man's position of power as he claims to be a vessel of God for the church and community. Abusive men may claim it's only wisdom to stay under their "umbrella of authority and protection," a medieval belief that under the care and concern of the leader his followers would be privileged to have his protection against harm. But for many, it is under this umbrella that proves to be the most vulnerable of places. The umbrella of authority and protection doubles as a scepter of fear and control.

Enabling

A particular crop of enablers do not necessarily grasp how their unwillingness to question or scrutinize the system and its leader wreaks havoc that is emotionally, financially, professionally, and spiritually damaging. They are willfully blind to any deviance behind closed doors, they celebrate only the wins that are fed to them. In an office setting, this could be low-level employees who lack direct contact with the abusive leader, shareholders who care only for the bottom line, or even upper management who trust their leader at all costs—despite red flags.

In the context of a church, this could be office staff who honor their leaders as enforced by scriptural edict and refuse to question the man of God, or parishioners who faithfully tithe to an organization that fails to ensure a workplace free of sexism and sexual misconduct. Both parties regularly provide standing ovations for the pastor's heartfelt sermons. Others, whom we might consider as the more assiduous enablers, knowingly allow misconduct to continue by writing payoff checks, underestimating the infractions of the abuser, choosing silence for fear of slander, and meticulously wiping email servers to hide the paper trail of transgressions.

Writing for the *Harvard Business Review*, Celia Swanson, Walmart's first female executive vice president, summarizes how enabling a toxic culture is both passive *and* active. "Passive enablers—which is what I was," Swanson writes, "are typically unaware of what's happening. They often mean well but are blinded by 'achievement mode' and are focused on driving results. They get to a point where they simply don't look further than they should and naively trust that their leaders are operating from their same value system and leadership style." By contrast, active enablers

> do see what is happening but fail to take action. They are crucial to combating toxic behavior because they are typically in the trenches of the problem and can best describe and document the situation. But they can be hesitant to speak up about what they are experiencing because they think they lack the status to bring a complaint forward or fear that there will be repercussions. They assume someone else will take a stand, rationalize that the situation may not be that bad, or delay action to wait for more proof to validate their uncertainty.[1]

At the same time, many women, myself included, have felt trapped in an honor culture that heralds loyalty as the supreme manifestation of holiness. It may feel like a fruitless effort to report misconduct, but it doesn't negate our obligation to bring to light indiscretions as a follower charged with exposing worthless deeds (Eph. 5:11). We fail the people in our world when we choose silence, never opting to raise a fuss. We play what we believe to be our role in the kingdom. In reality, we empower a broken empire.

Motivations

Enabling emotional, spiritual, psychological, and sexual abuse at a woman's expense isn't necessarily overt, where one may nod their head and say, "Oh, yes, that behavior is definitely enabling a pervert, and it must stop!" The actions of enablers are nuanced, complicated, and motivated by what they have to gain or lose in the situation. Active enablers falsely assume an air of innocence because there was no action taken on their part to directly harm someone else, only to cover it up, but their agreement to abuse others was indirect and often repeated over and over. For Christians, adhering to misinterpreted Scripture that venerates a spiritual leader only furthers their willingness to passively or actively enable. It ensures that the suffering continue to suffer, and the powerful continue to reign. Allowing a comment to slide, looking the other way when we witness indiscretion, downplaying misconduct, paying off accusers, or vehemently defending a predator all clearly constitute enabling, and many of us enable without a clear idea of the societal consequences when we do. Our own conscience is compromised when we remain silent in our convictions, and in the case of silencing and slandering women, staying quiet leads to collective harm.

Considering silence to be a form of enabling is necessary because it illustrates that those with personal knowledge of harassment or misconduct did in fact have good reason to report but didn't and therefore bolstered the abuser's practices. Often, enablers are more concerned with staying on the side of power rather than fixing the broken system that enables the powerful to prey on the powerless. To report misconduct and demand accountability would ensure that enablers lose their own piece of the power pie. Enablers aren't blind to the antics of the abuser; they simply choose to overlook the immorality in favor of professional, personal, or perceived spiritual clout.

Enablers who fail to hold their leaders accountable often have power, money, or some measure of equity on the line. For Harvey Weinstein, it was his brother and business partner, Bob, who knew about Harvey's sexual crimes against women but who chose to keep it to himself, never demanding safety *before* women were harmed.[2] Why? Because they had built a multi-billion-dollar entertainment empire together. As Ronan Farrow, writing for the *New Yorker*, reports, "In one case, in the nineteen-nineties, Bob Weinstein, who cofounded the film studio Miramax with his brother, paid two hundred and fifty thousand pounds, roughly six hundred thousand dollars today, to be split between two female employees in England who accused Harvey Weinstein of sexual harassment and assault. The funds came from Bob Weinstein's personal bank account—a move that helped conceal the payment from executives at Miramax and its parent company, Disney, as well as from Harvey Weinstein's spouse."[3]

Accomplices who enable a predator aren't always close confidants. In the case of musician R. Kelly, Jim DeGrotis (a Chicago journalist who chronicled Kelly's career for decades) believes that the number of people who knew about or witnessed the damage Kelly caused was likely in the thousands—employees at record labels, recording studios, publicity firms, and music venues, in addition to Kelly's team of assistants, lawyers, managers, drivers, and security guards. Those who by their inaction enabled Kelly's abusive behavior toward women and girls ranged from the richest producers in the music industry to hourly employees working on set as production assistants for his music videos, yet all, arguably, were motivated by money and a coveted place within the pop-culture hierarchy. DeGrotis claims that those who knew of Kelly's abuse of underage girls "allowed him to continue, because he was a musical genius, an artist, and (perhaps most important) a lucrative hit maker."[4]

Again, an active enabler's concern is to stay on the side of power, even if the power is corrupt. Benefiting from a predator's abuse of power, however material or abstract, is enough motivation to hide, minimize, or deflect the sins of the accused, and there is no room to claim innocence. Not if one is a member of the clergy, a brother to a Hollywood executive, a music producer, or an employee at one of the nation's most esteemed academic establishments.

With reputations to uphold, educational institutions across the country have failed to follow appropriate protocol when sexual assault was reported on campus grounds for fear that their polished image would be tarnished and that potential students would look elsewhere for post-secondary education. In the past, rather than file police reports or adhere to the federal antidiscrimination law under Title IX of the Education Amendments of 1972, universities have settled for confidential mediation or minimal and even nonexistent consequences for perpetrators on campus. This plays out in practice when, say, the person who has been harassed or assaulted still has to attend Biology 201 with her abuser if she wants to graduate from the school she fought to get into, and there is nothing she can do about it. She's probably already tried.

Christine Hauser, writing for the *New York Times*, reported that "In 2014, Harvard was one of more than 50 colleges and universities under investigation by the United States Education Department, accused of violating federal laws related to sexual assault complaints."[5] The Obama administration pushed for much-needed policy changes and threatened to withhold funds from the top university and college campuses in the country, including Ivy League schools such as Dartmouth and Princeton, private schools like Boston University and the University of Southern California, and public universities including Florida State, the University of Michigan, Ohio State, and Penn State if they did not implement adequate sexual misconduct policies.[6]

Yet, ten months after Donald Trump's election, this demand for policies was reversed by the Department of Education's Office for Civil Rights.[7] Powerful educational institutions reclaimed their ability to silence accusers and hide misconduct. Undoubtedly, the silencing nature of universities enables abusers to carry fraternity culture into adult life. Men who escaped consequences for their actions as students at the nation's top universities think themselves immune from consequences. A student at Vanderbilt University's Business School summed it up perfectly: "It's arrogance mixed with the feeling of invincibility."[8]

Women Enabling Men

In my experience, nothing singes the skin more than other women—who may have been considered friends and who were steeped in the same sexualized culture together—who decimate the character of a silence breaker and dismiss the actions of a predator in an attempt to protect their positions. These women, perhaps, did not interpret the predator's personal behavior toward them to be reprehensible, despite others in their immediate sphere experiencing harassment or worse. They likely did not experience what vocal victims experienced, yet rather than considering how misconduct could have taken place, they offer an alternative narrative, one that undercuts the validity of the silence breaker. While it is expected for an accused man to have defenders, a defense by other women close to the situation proves particularly painful as it pits the testimonies of women against each other. Silence breakers expect blowback from a narcissistic power abuser for exposing his behavior, but the swift defense from other women to protect him and inadvertently belittle the victim's testimony is patriarchy at its peak.

For men who abuse their power, women make the perfect puppets. When accusations are reported to superiors, the enablers who have been conditioned to downplay poor treatment act just as puppets tethered to a puppet master would. They defend a "good" man. They corroborate the telling of his story, defend his character, and do their best to ensure he comes out looking rather kind-hearted. They deliver testimonies praising the alleged offender's demeanor and personal conduct. Of course those who witnessed odd behavior and minimized its effects will praise the offender; they will appear culpable otherwise.

It is jarring that grown women, despite knowledge of an abuser's predatory behavior, enable and defend a male predator and turn their backs on their female colleagues and friends. Yet it's an effective way to lock down the position and place of power they have proximity to. It happens in every system in modern society—the rules of patriarchy are entrenched in the female brain in such a profound way that women support and protect men at all costs, ignoring their judgment and denying their own needs, agency, and sense of self. They uphold their place and decimate dissenters, because complicity is rewarded and resistance is shamed.

In 2016, Fox News media titan Roger Ailes was sued by Gretchen Carlson for sexual misconduct. According to the *New York Times*, Carlson, a longtime Fox on-air personality, was subjected to Ailes's sexual harassment and was effectively fired after her employment contract wasn't renewed.[9] In the wake of the reports, several women defended Ailes, regardless of Carlson's recorded conversations with Ailes as evidence. Although many women at Fox News claimed it was common knowledge that Ailes was a creep, preying on young women with a promise to mentor them if they played his sexually charged games, it was women in that *same* office who claimed he was innocent.

Fox News host Greta Van Susteren went on to dismiss Carlson as "a very unhappy employee that lost her job." If there was something amiss with Ailes, Van Susteren was positive she would have known about it. "If there were something weird going on . . . at every business they gossip. I would have heard it. That would be brought to me. Likely because I've been there the longest and one of the oldest," Van Susteren said. "I certainly would have heard about it."[10]

"This is a man who champions women," Kimberly Guilfoyle, cohost of *The Five*, shared in an interview with *TVNewser.*[11] Martha MacCallum, coanchor of *America's Newsroom*, said in an interview, "Roger is such a terrific boss. I don't like to see anything that reflects negatively on him. If anything, [Carlson's lawsuit] sort of bonded us. It's brought people together."[12] Sandra Smith, cohost of *Outnumbered,* said in an interview with the *Hollywood Reporter,* "If I ever felt like I was working in a hostile environment, I wouldn't be here."[13]

When a puppet—actively or passively—enables a powerful man who has been the source of her power, she can appear almost righteous, daring to do the "right" thing by standing by the accused. But in the end, when the dark deeds are exposed to the light, enablers bear responsibility for allowing the puppet master to destroy those in his path. Those who enable by unfairly giving the benefit of the doubt without any questioning, or by hiding misconduct, or by slandering silence breakers, may feel justified for protecting a predator, but in fact, they preserve the cycle of abuse and fortify the patriarchy.

Women who've been silenced desperately need others, especially other women, to unite *for* them rather *against* them. We need to remember that all men and woman are broken, capable of reprehensible behavior. It invites an examination of the heart, as exhibited by the psalmist in Psalm 139:23–24, "Search me, God, and know my heart; test me and know my anxious thoughts. See if there is any offensive way in me, and lead me in the way everlasting." Inviting the Lord to reveal the inner workings of our hearts sets the stage to reveal how we may have actively or passively enabled injustice or caused the harmed undue suffering by our defense of men in power.

"The politics of patriarchy is the politics of domination," note Carol Gilligan and Naomi Snider, authors of *Why Does Patriarchy Persist?*[14] In families, economies, churches, and cultures around the world, patriarchal traditions that men preach and women comply with will always be at odds with gospel liberation when women are silenced after undue harm. We must resist. Even more, when white supremacy organizes the voices of the victimized, leaving women of color at the end of the line to fight patriarchal power, this is what activist Rachel Cargle calls "white supremacy in heels."[15] During the suffrage movement, Black women were relegated to the back of the march while fighting for the vote as they fought for their rights as people of color. White women took the lead, prioritizing their needs over their marginalized sisters' needs.[16] White women, especially resourced white women, must act to ensure marginalized women—low-wage earning, immigrant, undocumented, Black, indigenous, Asian, Latina—do not suffer unspeakable harm as they secure liberation from patriarchal injustice.

As followers of Jesus, we are invited to be ambassadors of justice for the suffering, not pawns for patriarchal power players. The wisdom of Proverbs 22:8 reminds us, "Whoever sows injustice reaps calamity, and the rod they wield in fury will be broken." The power used in fury to enable, to protect, and to posture will be broken when seeds of injustice are planted, and the fruit of enabling and deception will harm our own souls, uplift patriarchy, and keep women oppressed. Yet the way of Jesus and justice lifts a banner of love and care over the suffering, inviting us to draw near to the brokenhearted, and bear one another's burdens and so fulfill the law of Christ (Gal. 6:2). The way of Jesus does not allow us to sit idly by, to turn away in the midst of misconduct, no matter where we land in the pecking order. Instead, he invites us to be the good news to the harmed ones, to the ones slandered and punished for that which they did not bring upon themselves. Not puppets of the patriarchy but vessels of compassion.

8

LOOK AT WHO I AM

What has sadly become an acceptable rebuttal to a woman's claims of harassment and systemic silencing is for the accused to refute claims of *what* he's done with *who* he is and what he has accomplished. After claiming innocence or ignorance, he'll drum up adoration by his fans as he proudly stands on his public persona. As adorers recall and affirm accolades to bankroll support, the accused will credit himself as the victim of vicious attacks and maintain that his character would never stoop so low as to objectify, harass, or abuse a woman. He will feed any and all belief that he is in fact a good man incapable of abusing his power, and you or I might believe it. Jeff Dion, deputy executive director of the National Center for Victims of Crime, explains, "Perpetrators will set themselves up as pillars of society to hold themselves above reproach. People might go out of their way to establish themselves as charitable, compassionate . . . so that when an allegation does come up, that's their first line of defense."[1] A beloved public persona makes it seem impossible for a man to abuse his power at a woman's expense, so instead we doubt her.

In cases of sexual harassment and the systemic institutional harm it causes, we doubt a woman's experience because we want to believe a man's word. Could a woman's telling of her experience be true if the man she accuses of misconduct is beloved by all? What if he is someone who regularly wins the approval and respect of others? What if he has a faithful wife and devoted children? What if he has a track record of professional success? What if he has invested in his community in such a grand way that onlookers can trace positive results and achievements back to him? What if his adorers are convinced he wrote the book on women's empowerment? Surely his actions were misinterpreted or a crazed woman is out to get him, because a good man would never do what the accusers claim he did, right? Researchers aptly call this refusal to believe that "good" people are capable of bad things the "halo effect."

Writing for the *Economist*, Tim Hindle notes that the halo effect "is the phenomenon whereby we assume that because people are good at doing A they will be good at doing B, C and D (or the reverse—because they are bad at doing A they will be bad at doing B, C and D). If we see a person first in a good light, it is difficult subsequently to darken that light. The old adage that 'first impressions count' seems to be true."[2] Although previously mentioned, it bears repeating that men who abuse their power are often masters at positive first impressions. A charming persona, promise of upward movement, and kind gestures set the tone for how they are perceived by others. If the man who made a remarkable first impression on you shrewdly followed it up with emotional, relational, or spiritual availability, it makes perfect sense that any subsequent thought or action by him would be seen through rose-colored glasses, and how can you see red flags through rose-colored glasses? You can't. Richard Shweder, professor of human development at the University of Chicago, expands on why the halo effect is so powerful: "The mind mines the world for information to confirm preexisting beliefs. People strive to avoid the difficulty of reconciling conflicting information and hope to feel confident in their initial judgments."[3] If we deem someone as "good" from the start, it will take solid evidence to convince us otherwise. Even then, the human mind finds it incredibly difficult to swim upstream against the current of powerful first impressions.

The halo effect is exceptionally advantageous for a man who abuses his power behind closed doors because supporters must overcome their initial approval of him in order to assess his actions without partiality. Yet, more often than not, those charged with appraising the situation and assigning consequences employ confirmation bias, which is defined as "the human tendency to search for, favor, and use information that confirms one's pre-existing views on a certain topic."[4] Whereas the halo effect describes the internal struggle to believe someone deemed as "good" is in reality capable of doing harm, confirmation bias explains why staunch defendants cherry-pick situations and encounters to ensure their beloved leader, whether he is a politician, power broker, restaurant owner, factory floor manager, or pastor, remains in unsullied power.

A prime example of this is when famed victim's rights lawyer Lisa Bloom suggested an intentional release of photos featuring accusers smiling as they stood next to Harvey Weinstein as evidence to the public that Weinstein was innocent. Bloom surmised that if any woman were truly a victim of sexual harassment and assault, would she then pose for a photo with her assailant? Bloom's insinuation that victims wouldn't pose smiling with him was the kind of social proof necessary to confirm beliefs that Weinstein wasn't a predator but a promoter of women in the entertainment industry.[5]

Many defenders of a perpetrator attempt to deflate the narrative of silence breakers by explaining away the actions of the man in question, perhaps he was just *too* generous with his phone number, *too* caring and *too* kind with his availability toward the women around him, and those women likely misunderstood his kindness for come-ons. In their minds, how could anyone fault an emotionally available man who believed in the empowerment of women in the workplace? At the gym? Or in the church? Defenders claim that far too many women cry wolf over sexual harassment and assault, and they couldn't conceive how he would ever survive false allegations, despite the especially low rate of false reports.[6] Even worse, defenders justify their position of unwavering support by claiming that no one does as much good in the world as their guy. It is inconceivable for them to believe a good man is capable of such villainy. Regardless of what women said he did, they bank on who he said he was. It is difficult to sway someone's belief despite logic or evidence when they are emotionally attached to an offender. Emotional ties prove stronger than evidence when you desperately want to doubt a woman's testimony.

Clearly, subtle aspects of human psychology are at play when an offender is believed despite credible evidence justifying a woman's testimony against him. Research suggests that even the attractiveness of an offender works against the victim, as we tend to respect the account of attractive and successful people more than those who are not attractive and successful. But what is beautiful is not always good.[7]

As if the bravery of silence breakers who come forward to report is not sufficient reason to investigate and review any and all allegations, many defenders conclude that a perpetrator's accusers were trapped in rocky marriages, desperate for attention, or drunk and deranged. Due to the blatant instability of the accusing women, they reason, there is no credible rationale to believe their stories warrant an ounce of merit, thus substantiating the testimony of the accused, which proves his guiltlessness.

Character Defamation

If a victim makes headway in her healing, outing her perpetrator and discovering other victims along the way, progress has been made, but the perpetrator can hit back and punish his victims by slapping them with a lawsuit for character defamation. Since 2017, character defamation suits have been on the rise as women have stepped forward to tell the truth of their experience at the hands of powerful men. Pamela Lopez, a lobbyist in California who represents school districts, indigenous tribes, and interest groups, shared in *Mother Jones*, "I had to make my peace with recognizing that if I wanted to be a significant actor in politics, and work in the political world, that putting up with abusive behavior, putting up with sexism and sexual harassment by some men, was just part of the cost of doing business."

Yet, when the 2017 #MeToo reckoning tore through every sector of society, she signed an open letter denouncing the sexist behavior of men in California politics. According to the *Los Angeles Times*, after signing the letter, Lopez decided to go public with her story of how state assembly member Matt Dababneh in January 2016 pushed her into a bathroom, masturbated in front of her, and pressed her to touch him.[8] After her story was released, she was encouraged to file a formal complaint along with another victim of Dababneh, Jessica Yas Barker. After their complaint was filed in December 2017, three more women came forward accusing Dababneh of harassment and assault. Dababneh denied all allegations, but he did resign from his position, claiming that the truth would prevail once an assembly investigation was completed. After the investigation, in which "Lopez's story was 'more likely than not' accurate," the assembly committee refused Dababneh's request for an appeal. The women in the case had been heard, but Dababneh wasn't having it.

Not ten months later, Dababneh sued Lopez for character defamation, claiming that because of Lopez he suffered emotional damages—"anguish, fright, horror, nervousness, grief, anxiety, worry, shock, humiliation, and depression."[9] Lopez had a newborn, was in the process of purchasing a home, and faced the dread of mounting legal bills as she prepared to relive the hellish moment.

Defamation lawsuits, a legal response to misconduct allegations, are increasingly common as men of means attempt to defend their names and at the same time punish their accusers by demanding recompense. Defamation lawsuits can appear heroic as someone who is innocent would not sit silently by as they're besmirched by accusers, but many times it reveals deep-seated anger coupled with abusive power fueled by deep pockets. Strategic Lawsuits Against Public Participation (SLAPP) are of growing popularity among all sectors—clergy, business, athletics, education, medicine, politics—and uniquely reverse the role of victim and offender, a response known as the DARVO theory (deny, attack, and reverse victim and offender) developed by Jennifer Freyd, professor of psychology at the University of Oregon.[10] Research suggests that recasting roles using the DARVO method has the potential to lead bystanders to blame the accuser.

In response to a sharp increase of defamation lawsuits, anti-SLAPP laws in thirty states prevent defendants from advancing too far down the legal trail before the lawsuits are thrown out; however, accusers are still forced to fund the battle even if their claims prove true. Sharyn Tejani, director of the Time's Up Legal Defense Fund, which aids workplace harassment victims by covering a portion of legal bills, notes, "The threat of being sued, and the expense of mounting a legal defense, has deterred many survivors who seek to speak out—not to mention the stress of rehashing traumatic events in court."[11] In some instances, even the threat of litigation is enough to convince those close to the situation that an alleged offender has been subject to vicious attacks by women out to get him. Defamation suits rarely go to trial, but for supporters of the offender, they serve as social proof that he is innocent and willing to fight for his name.

But I'm Powerful

If all else fails, the accused may offer an admission of guilt with just a splash of ignorance. Looking as though you misunderstand how you come off to others can prove useful in eliciting sympathy when other options have been exhausted. It's simply another way to cast suspicion on the validity of a woman's experience while providing the accused the benefit of the doubt, excusing his intent despite its detrimental impact. A prime example of this in recent history are the claims made by women who felt the hugs and kisses offered by Joe Biden prior to his election to the office of president of the United States were inappropriate and made them feel uncomfortable.

According to the *New York Times*, while speaking at an International Brotherhood of Electrical Workers conference in Washington, Biden quasi-apologized for his physical contact with women by stating, "I'm sorry I didn't understand more" in response to reporter's questions about his hugs and kisses to women over the years. "I'm not sorry for any of my intentions. I'm not sorry for anything that I have ever done. I've never been disrespectful intentionally to a man or a woman." Later in his talk, as he hugged those who approached the stage, he jokingly commented that he was given consent to physically hug the women who introduced him and the boys who joined him at the podium.[12] Biden's flippant comments *after* his depthless apology undercut his atonement for his signature actions with women and minimized the experience of any woman whom Biden made to feel uncomfortable. His power afforded him such a position.

By now we understand that power unequivocally plays a role in what many male leaders believe is appropriate or inappropriate as they relate to the women around them. They are fit to define what a woman deserves from them, and as the access to power increases, research reveals, so does many men's hunger for domination of the weaker sex. Psychology professor Dacher Keltner notes in the *Harvard Business Review*, "Powerful men, studies show, overestimate the sexual interest of others and erroneously believe that the women around them are more attracted to them than is actually the case. Powerful men also sexualize their work, looking for opportunities for sexual trysts and affairs, and along the way leer inappropriately, stand too close, and touch for too long on a daily basis, thus crossing the lines of decorum—and worse." Keltner makes the case "that abuses of power are both predictable and recurring" and in an experiment where those who felt powerful were monitored, researchers discovered that "they develop empathy deficits and are less able to read others' emotions and take others' perspectives. And they behave in an impulsive fashion—they violate the ethics of the workplace."[13]

Such was the case for law professor Anita Hill, when in October 1991, seventeen years before Christine Blasey Ford went through her round of questioning before Congress, she testified against Supreme Court judge nominee Clarence Thomas after he allegedly harassed her when he served as her supervisor at the Department of Education and the Equal Employment Opportunity Commission (EEOC; the very organization charged with investigating harassment and discrimination in privately owned workplaces, nonprofit organizations, and government agencies across the country). Hill, a Black woman, sat before an all-white, all-male Senate Judiciary Committee, detailing Thomas's crude behavior on national television. According to Hill's claims, "Judge Thomas had repeatedly asked her to go out with him in a social capacity and would not take no for an answer. She said he would talk about sex in vivid detail, describing pornography he had seen involving women with large breasts, women having sex with animals, group sex and rape scenes. Judge Thomas would also talk about his own 'sexual prowess' in workplace conversations." Although Hill was the only one who testified, another witness could have publicly corroborated her story. Angela Wright, a former public affairs officer from the EEOC, was prepared to take the stand and testify that Judge Thomas had pressured her to date him, but she never had a chance to testify. Wright's testimony, which was similar to Hill's own experience, proves Keltner's theory—powerful men overestimate the desire others have for them, and their abusive power patterns are reoccurring. But of course, despite the testimony of Hill, a respected law professor, Thomas was confirmed by the Senate 52 to 48, winning a seat on the highest court in the land.[14]

Clarence Thomas exerted his power over Hill when he claimed that the hearings over Hill's accusations were "a national disgrace." He dubbed his experience "a high-tech lynching for uppity blacks who in any way deign to think for themselves, to do for themselves, to have different ideas." By centering his defense on race, Thomas swerved the conversation away from allegations of sexual misconduct to a Senate-sponsored racial attack, which undermined Hill's identity, both her susceptibility to harassment and the believability of her accusations. At work was misogynoir, a term coined by Moya Bailey, a postdoctoral fellow at Northeastern University. Misogynoir cites the unique way African American women face anti-Black racism and misogyny simultaneously.[15] As explained earlier, the intersectionality of race and gender leaves marginalized women vulnerable in ways not experienced by white women, but misogynoir builds on the systemic racism that chronically denigrates a Black woman's experience.

When asked by *Essence* in 2016 how race and gender affected how she was received by an all-male, all-white Senate committee, Hill noted, "Those members of Congress had never even considered that Black women had our own political voice. They assumed that Black men spoke for us. For an African American woman to have her own political voice and own political position, and to believe that our perspective should be added to the conversation, was just something they hadn't even considered."[16] Judge Thomas maintained a position of power amid the hearings, but Hill, by her presence, position, and testimony, challenged the notion that women "ask for it" or must comply with unjust environments devised by powerful men. Despite the label of "race traitor" and threats of rape, sodomy, and murder for speaking up, Hill bravely professed before the senators, "It would have been more comfortable to remain silent, but when I was asked by a representative of this committee to report my experience, I felt that I had to tell the truth. I could not keep silent."[17]

Throughout history, women overwhelmingly have been silenced when they've had a truth to tell, so much so that it felt detrimental to speak up. A waste of words. Yet Jesus, who came to make all things right, who came to overthrow power structures that demean and oppress, gave women a voice when others didn't. He dignified their experiences by his actions and attention and invited women to take their place as beloved daughters.

For the bleeding woman who was plagued by her condition for twelve years, he stopped a crowd to acknowledge her faith and healing (Luke 8:43–48). After Jesus asked who touched the hem of his garment, she courageously spoke up to tell what had happened, even though her actions—an unclean woman grasping on to a man, a rabbi no less—broke the law and could have led to grave consequences for this already suffering woman. Jesus called her, a woman ostracized by her community due to her condition, a "daughter." She was not the dirty, unclean woman. She was a daughter. For the woman quite literally bleeding to death, he stopped the bleeding and honored her faith. He made space for her voice and her experience. He welcomed the interruption to engage a woman in need, and he still does.

For the woman at the well, a Samaritan woman who sat alone at Jacob's well at perhaps the hottest hour of the day, Jesus dismissed the practices of the day (Jews not associating with Samaritans, men engaging women only if their husbands were present), recognized her losses, and offered what a husband could not (John 4:1–42). In a time when a husband represented a voice, a place, security, means, and protection, she had none. Yet after her encounter with Jesus, she dropped her bucket and raised her voice to all who would listen to tell of the man "who told me everything I ever did" (4:39). Because of Jesus, this woman spoke up to the very people she was likely trying to avoid.

Not only did Jesus give women a voice, he protected them—their bodies and their reputations. For the woman caught in adultery, he first and foremost chose to protect her (John 7:53–8:11). He did not wait until he got to the bottom of the issue, finding out exactly what she had done, if she had been seduced, if there was a power imbalance, or if she started it. Ensuring her safety came first. After he wrote in the sand and dared others to cast the first stone, he spoke to her compassionately. He was not another man who would take advantage of her. Although Jesus told her to "Go and sin no more," he did not condemn her. He was the man who protected her.

Instead of doubting women and listening only to men in power report the narrative, Jesus models for us all a response to a woman with a truth to tell who has been hurt by another and harmed by her community. He doesn't ask the woman caught in adultery if she asked for it, what she wore, or if she led on the man she slept with. He doesn't accuse the woman at the well of internal brokenness that invited desertion by men who would care for her. He doesn't dismiss the bleeding woman because of her social standing. To all these women and more, he dignifies their experiences, offers compassion, and displays to onlookers the care and respect she is worthy of. We can do the same.

We are told by those bent on hiding misconduct and by fear in our minds that silence in the midst of misconduct appears to be the smartest and arguably the most spiritual response, but Jesus makes it clear by his actions, words, and care for women that silence is not spiritual; it's destructive, isolating, and anti-gospel.

PART 3

HOW EVERYONE CAN SPEAK UP

The function of freedom is to free someone else.

—TONI MORRISON, COMMENCEMENT
SPEECH AT BARNARD COLLEGE, 1979

9

ALLIES

Allyship with women isn't limited to marching in the streets and digital activism on Twitter, although that is helpful, necessary, and needed. Allyship requires both introspection and intentional actions that ensure women have safe, dignified opportunities to work, play, and simply exist by dismantling archaic systems that leave women vulnerable to harm. Demolishing a culture of complicity is not a top-down exercise; it's an every-single-one-of-us exercise. We can all serve as allies who lend support to the victimized and become advocates when we take action in the face of uncertainty, sacrificing our own place and power in the system.

To serve as an active ally first requires examining our place within our given hierarchy, asking ourselves: How do I benefit from silence? What power, or proximity to power, do I possess that would cause me to defend a powerful man faced with accusations? What do I believe about a woman's place in my world? How have my past experiences, education, faith, exposure to media, and family of origin shaped my understanding of women's rights? Have I allowed the Scriptures, which regard men and women as equal, to instruct my human-ity, or has my humanity, geography, political preference, or religious affiliation instructed my beliefs about what women should endure? How have I, as a man or woman, elevated my *potential* response to harassment or abuse above victims' responses? How have I supported pastors, politicians, policies, and people in power who've abused their power but deny it's an issue? How do I feel about the powerful people's treatment of women in the places I work or worship?

Dismantling any ounce of foul thinking that would cause us to silence women is vital in serving as an ally. As we address our internal ideologies and biases, we can identify and seek safe systems that dignify women. Women alone cannot do this. It will take a deliberate and sustained contribution from men, an effort that is long overdue. Men, undeniably, have a unique role to play to move toward a balance of power between men and women and to serve as allies to women who've been harmed.

Gendered oppression will continue so long as women are the ones tasked with solving the issue, when in reality this issue exists in large part due to abuse of power rooted in toxic masculinity, not weak femininity. This issue is a man's issue as much as it is a woman's issue, if not more so. It is decidedly not enough for men to not harass, assault, silence, slander, and destroy women. Allyship demands assessing the gendered hierarchy present in nearly every system and how men have consciously or subconsciously played a role that keeps them as first and women as second. Values of equality grate against misogyny, and even good men unintentionally perpetuate a broken system that demeans and objectifies women. But it doesn't have to be this way. Male allyship for gendered equality is possible. Writing for the *Harvard Business Review*, psychology professor W. Brad Johnson and sociology professor David G. Smith define male allyship as members of an advantaged group committed to building relationships with women, expressing as little sexism in their own behavior as possible, understanding the social privilege conferred by their gender, and demonstrating active efforts to address gender inequities at work and in society.[1] Male allyship suggests that men have an active and involved role to support women that is only theirs to offer.

While desperately needed, male allyship isn't always easy to navigate. According to research, in many cases gender-egalitarian men are treated as if they are weak by other men *and* women as they pursue collaboration among genders rather than assuming a patriarchal disposition.[2] Their allyship efforts are misunderstood, and they are seen as preferring women over men. On the flipside, they may experience the Pedestal Effect,[3] a term coined by Tal Peretz, a professor at Auburn University, to describe how men are given special treatment for small acts of gender equality such as hiring a female employee or allowing a woman to preach a Sunday sermon. Male allyship requires an examination of patriarchy's deep roots and intentionally decentering male privilege to better understand and come alongside women. Author Susan Brownmiller notes in her book *Against Our Will*, "Concepts of hierarchy, slavery, and private property flowed from, and could only be predicated upon, the initial subjugation of woman."[4] Throughout history, men have conquered women for their own benefit and advantage, and it will take more than virtue signaling or promoting women as tokens to powerful positions to ensure women are seen and treated as equals, especially in moments when women have been silenced.

As men decenter their "superior" experience, address their male fragility, and consider women's "inferior" experiences, they can use their position, voice, influence, and pocketbook to further a balance of power between men and women, while giving up any notion that they are the true victims of the #MeToo movement. They can address and eradicate systemic limits placed on women while also recognizing and confronting their abuse of power, if even in the most minute of ways. Writing for *Harper's Bazaar*, Jennifer Wright notes, "Eliminating institutional barriers and yet continuing to allow harassment is akin to welcoming a woman into an office filled with scorpions."[5] Put plainly, theory must be put into practice—in the boardroom, newsroom, prayer room, and especially amid the locker-room banter. Men can and must do better.

For men to serve as an ally, when women share how they've been trapped in a no-win cycle where they feel they have no choice but to comply with sexist standards that belittle their personhood, men must empathetically listen to these experiences without dismissing them, and without defense, interruptions, or mansplaining. As men listen and learn, they can identify with a humble heart how misogyny manifests itself and how harassment plays out in reality, and they can discover what is needed from women to ensure they can thrive within their context. As men gain intel, it is for the sole intent and purpose of partnering with women for their much-deserved place in the system, never to exploit their loyalty. Rather than waiting until women come seeking solutions, men should pursue understanding and equality at their own expense.

For male allyship to move from apathetic to aware to active to advocating,[6] men must not assume they know what women need but keep an open-door policy to learn, build trust and rapport, and understand how their best efforts can be utilized to ensure a dignified place and space for the women in their world. If presented an opportunity for advancement, men can recommend opportunities be redirected to capable women who are as deserving of the position, job, or platform. It's mens' brains, not necessarily their brawn, that are required to build equitable and dignified spaces for men *and* women. As issues arise, men can glean from the trusted female relationships before they use their voice to defend, speak up, or upset the system. Where there is male allyship, there is less likely to be silence, slander, and shame heaped on victims by abusive men in power, because the bar for what is acceptable is simply higher as men are compelled to respect and dignify women's marginalized experiences.

We Need More Nathans

The Lord sent Nathan to David. When he came to him, he said, "There were two men in a certain town, one rich and the other poor. The rich man had a very large number of sheep and cattle, but the poor man had nothing except one little ewe lamb he had bought. He raised it, and it grew up with him and his children. It shared his food, drank from his cup and even slept in his arms. It was like a daughter to him.

"Now a traveler came to the rich man, but the rich man refrained from taking one of his own sheep or cattle to prepare a meal for the traveler who had come to him. Instead, he took the ewe lamb that belonged to the poor man and prepared it for the one who had come to him."

David burned with anger against the man and said to Nathan, "As surely as the LORD lives, the man who did this must die! He must pay for that lamb four times over, because he did such a thing and had no pity."

Then Nathan said to David, "You are the man!" (2 Sam. 12:1–7a)

To right the cultural wrongs in our day, we would all be wise to pursue silence breaking as did Nathan, a male ally to Bathsheba in 2 Samuel 12 after she was sexually assaulted by David. It was Nathan who spoke up against the evil act David committed and outlined the king's consequences as ordained by God. Nathan was a trusted court prophet who was attuned to the way of the Father and spoke the truth. He was not a gossip, nor was he a rabble rouser. He was working for the good, not against it. Today it's the modern-day Nathans who bravely speak truth to power, not to usurp leadership but to bring correction and healing.

Rather than speak up and clearly communicate with conviction, as Nathan did, in some faith contexts the spiritual advisers of our day have taken the shepherds who've abused their power and have moved them from church to church and parish to parish. Without the sharing between institutions of their knowledge of past indiscretions, perpetrators are awarded hefty severances to disappear. Preservation of the perpetrator is the goal—zip the lips of the accuser, applaud the predator upon his grand exit, send the perpetrator to a new post, line his pockets with cash, and allow the church to keep up appearances. He isn't repentant. He's relocated.

To excuse harassment and assault, well-meaning men and women may assert that "it's just how men are," reinforcing an archaic, misogynistic, patriarchal rationale that claims men must conquer and women must be emotionally and sexually conquered, which leaves the victims silenced by their perpetrator and the system that enabled him. "There's an understanding [among evangelicals] that God designed men to be natural sexual initiators," says Samuel Perry, professor of religious studies at the University of Oklahoma. "Being an evangelical man and confessing to being somebody who makes sexual mistakes almost validates your masculinity," he argues. "It's indicative of, 'Look, I'm a man, I'm a red-blooded man who struggles with sin like everybody else. And I'm dealing with it.'"[7]

In reality, regardless of whatever excuse a man caught in sin offers, there should still be repercussions. When Nathan confronted King David, David did not list off excuses as to why he was entitled to sin against Bathsheba, nor did he twist the story to vindicate himself. He was wrong, and his actions were identified as wrong. Nathan did not downplay or justify

David's actions. He called it as it was. As we look for modern-day Nathans, allies who step up to break the silence when misconduct is swept under the rug, call out abuse for what it is and who it harms, and hold perpetrators accountable for their wrongdoing, we can demand that appropriate consequences are delivered to the offender, even if it's someone who has pastored us or employs us so that we can pay our bills.

For many women of faith, their experience of abuse isn't appropriately named or addressed, which only further harms. Rather than seek safety and distance from unhealthy persons, in many congregations Christian women are encouraged to stay in an abusive environment even after they've reported it to church leaders or lay counselors. The preoccupation with the family unit as the apex of Christian life plays into this narrative that woman should, at all costs, remain in a toxic environment because God abhors divorce and a woman's place is at the side of a man. Women have been bullied into silent suffering by those who should serve as their closest allies. Allyship has never been more critical to God's redemptive plan for humanity, as patriarchal beliefs continue to silence women desperate for mental, emotional, physical, and spiritual safety. If we glean insight from David's encounter with Nathan, we see that a right response from an advocate would involve belief in the woman sharing her experience; naming the harassment or assault; a swift rebuke of the abuse; a call to the police, if needed, to report the crime committed; and protection and compassionate care for the victim of abuse, not thoughts and prayers alone.

In any case of abuse, a quiet plea for repentance from the perpetrator and an offer of forgiveness from spiritual leadership does *not* nullify the need for justice in matters of misconduct. The criminal justice system is not at odds with the church but is a necessary means of justice and accountability when abuse arises within church communities. Churches are not equipped to adjudicate claims where the law has been broken, which is why it is imperative that church leaders, whether it reflects poorly on the church or not, contact governing authorities who are equipped to convict abusers, determine consequences, and prevent further abuse. Encouraging women to tolerate even an ounce of abuse, and then insisting on exclusively handling it within church walls rather than reporting it to the authorities, leaves women defenseless and with no avenue for compassionate care and healing. As allies, we have the opportunity to speak up for truth, mercy, and justice, just as Nathan did.

Silence Is Not Spiritual, Helpful, or Good for Anyone

As bystanders and institutions consider potential losses—professional, personal, communal, and financial—that they assume inhibit their ability to act on behalf of silenced women, they willfully withhold compassion from those who need it and defy the gospel call to care for the least among us. Perhaps they assume someone else will speak up, take up the cause, care for the victim, and stand as an ally while they sidestep the issue they intrinsically believe does not affect them. Yet, to right this cultural wrong, we must see ourselves as allies to silenced women, not bystanders who look the other way when we witness glaring warning signs.

Warning signs include the following:

- women who have been publicly or privately slandered by a man
- women who are constantly worried about making a powerful man angry
- women who excuse the behavior of a man with more power than they have
- a powerful man who is jealous, possessive, or manipulative to women

- powerful men who physically corner women
- powerful men who joke about women's bodies
- women who harbor fear of retaliation from a powerful man
- a severe change in mood or demeanor in a woman after having been with a powerful man

While most of us may not witness the abuse of power behind closed doors, we can see its effects with warning signs that may appear insignificant at first but point to an abuse of power. As warning signs are identified, it's imperative to remain gentle and compassionate and look to empower the woman who has been demeaned by a man's abuse of power. The goal is not to be a hero of her story but to be an empowered ally, a friend on her journey to justice and healing. But before the worst happens, research suggests there is a highly effective way to prevent sexual harassment, aptly called bystander intervention,[8] because the onus to act is not limited only to the preyed upon, human resource departments, university officials, church leaders, or the police, but includes everyone at the first sight of a physical or verbal power imbalance. Tactics for bystander intervention include the following:

Disrupt the situation: Get the person out of it or distract the harasser. Ask, "Do you want to go get lunch?" when a woman appears uncomfortable, or "Hey there, may I speak to you for a minute?" "Did you want to walk out of the office together?" "May I join you in here?" "Should we get going?" Even the slightest distraction could prevent harassment.

Confront the harasser: If appropriate and able, ask questions like, "Are you aware of how you were perceived in that situation?" "Did you see that?" "I don't think that's a good idea." "I don't think she took it like that?" "I know you probably didn't mean it, but it appeared to make her feel uncomfortable."

Check on her: Address the woman directly, offering care and concern, as well as a willingness to approach human resources, university counsel, church leaders, or whoever else in the system is charged with handling harassment.[9]

Jesus models this when he encounters the adulterous woman (John 7:53–8:11). As she is trapped by Pharisees and fears physical assault by public stoning, Jesus first disrupts the situation by writing in the sand as his answer to the question posed by the Pharisees, who intend to trap Jesus at the woman's expense. This ensures the woman's physical safety by his own presence and actions. Then he confronts her harassers. He dares them to cast the first stone if they are without sin. When she is safe, he engages her in conversation. The Scriptures lead us to believe he spoke to her with tenderness, care, and compassion. While Jesus's situation escalated quickly, it likely won't be that way for us, but we cannot underestimate our intervention, even if it seems insignificant.

As people of conviction, remaining silent as we dismiss the experiences of victims for any political, social, financial, or perceived spiritual gain is dangerous and indicative of systemic domination of women's bodies and testimonies. If we are to honor the basic dignity inherent in every human being, forgoing silence in matters of harassment, abuse, and institutional harm is the first act in caring for women who've been victimized. While it's easy to side with the perpetrator, who asks nothing of us *but* silence, it is altogether more demanding to listen to the truth from the mouths of the abused and allow belief to move us to action. There is no circumstance under heaven in which any man—not a powerbroker on Wall Street, pastor, college president, or politician—should be awarded a free pass for his misconduct. Excusing a "chosen" man's unwanted advances with our silence only bolsters the evangelical church's longstanding patriarchal honor culture that permeates faith spaces and harms all in its path.

With courage and commitment, women from across the church are speaking up against the disreputable way churches and believers have handled abuse and pledging to do better. Started by social justice advocates Belinda Bauman and Lisa Sharon Harper in December 2017, the #SilenceIsNotSpiritual movement gained momentum as men and women pledged "to stand with women who experience violence" as well as "to stand up for women who experience violence." The statement, with signatories from dozens of prominent Christian women, declared, "This moment in history is ours to steward. We are calling churches, particularly those in our stream of the Christian faith—Evangelical churches, to end the silence and stop all participation in violence against women. We call our pastors, our elders, and our parishioners who have been silent to speak up and stand up for all who experience abuse. There is no institution with greater capacity to create protected spaces for healing and restoration for survivors, as well as confession, repentance and rehabilitation for perpetrators."[10]

As allies, it is imperative we take note, stand up, engage ourselves in this demanding work of identifying abuse of power, and shoulder the heaviness that women experience at the hands of a perpetrator. We, as the body of Christ, should operate not as a harbor for unrepentant perpetrators that we defend but as a sanctuary of safety for the violated and suffering.

How we, as followers of Jesus, respond to the #MeToo and #ChurchToo movements will either invite victims of misconduct closer to Christ, who binds up the brokenhearted, or, whether we are well-intentioned or not, will turn us into the bystanders casting the first stone—shaming victims for their story of harassment and harm. This reckoning of our day is not only a time to clean house by calling out the rife sexual misconduct prevalent in our society but also a time to do what we, as believers, have been called to do: carry the burden with silenced victims who feel as though no one is coming to their aid, stand in the gap, hold them up, and walk with them as they heal.

Paul's words of encouragement in 2 Corinthians 1:3–5 tell us, "Praise be to the God and Father of our Lord Jesus Christ, the Father of compassion and the God of all comfort, who comforts us in all our troubles, so that we can comfort those in any trouble with the comfort we ourselves receive from God. For just as we share abundantly in the sufferings of Christ, so also our comfort abounds through Christ." With our strength, resolve, and comfort found in Christ, we can comfort those who've suffered unspeakable harm, sharing with them that they are not the sum of their experience. We can console victims by compassionately acknowledging the harm caused by abuse of power; this requires a refusal to minimize the effects of abuse. We can listen without judgment. We can make space for them to be seen, heard, and known. We can, as James instructs, "be quick to listen, slow to speak and slow to become angry" (1:19). We can consider our tone, facial expression, and comments as we look not to induce shame or retrigger trauma but communicate with honor and grace. We can build trust with our willingness to listen and pray as they process their experiences, and we can help them explore their options for healing and redress. We can resist comparing their trauma to another's and simply carry with them a burden no woman should ever have to carry on her own.

As Immanuel came to live among us, so we too can live and serve among the broken. In the parable of the good Samaritan (Luke 10:25–37), Jesus reveals that the righteous ones—the priest and the Levite—were guilty of withholding compassion and care from a suffering victim who had been beaten, robbed, and left for dead. It was a Samaritan (an ethnic identity despised by the Jews) who did not pass by but approached the victim in pain, had compassion on him, bound up his wounds, and poured on the victim his own oil and wine. He sacrificed his own animal to carry the victim to a place of safety and paid for the victim's stay until he was restored to health. The man who heard Jesus share this parable was told to go and do likewise. This is what loving your neighbor looks like: offering compassion to the suffering among us.

As a practice of Christian spirituality, we are to compassionately care for the hurting among us as demonstrated by the good Samaritan. Like any sacrifice, it comes with a price tag. It can cost us emotional, spiritual, financial, and societal equity to serve as a sacrificial Samaritan who operates with compassion and mercy rather than remaining a silent bystander. It recognizes the broken as our neighbor, as someone we are responsible to care for when she has been wronged. We must lend our strength, not cover our ears.

Jesus was not and is not threatened by loss of position, prestige, or access to power when he comforts those entrusted to him. The trappings of this world mean nothing to him, and he will not stay silent while women are harmed, slandered, and punished for telling the truth. As we follow him, imperfect though we are, we'll do right to remember that our call to comfort the vulnerable mirrors his in this upside-down kingdom, where the chosen ones in need of care and defense aren't found seated on the thrones of empire, but instead are found among the wounded crying out in lament.

In our day, the public lament of #MeToo stories is an invitation for all of us to mourn what's been stolen and lost. To sit in communal sorrow and ache for what has happened to our sisters, mothers, daughters, friends, and coworkers. It's an honest act that recognizes the agony that the harmed have endured and provides an opportunity for all of us to repent of our own complicity in the silencing of women. We can individually and collectively lament with the silenced rather than rationalize that if something really happened, they would have spoken up sooner or they should have kept it to themselves. When others cast stones, attempt to control the narrative, gaslight, or slander them, we can join the victimized in their outrage as committed allies over the damage done to their bodies, minds, and spirits. We can weep for their losses and cry out to God on their behalf for mercy and justice, not as a political act, but as a scriptural one that our fathers and mothers in the faith have practiced for centuries. From the sobs of our lament, may a clear cry for justice resound louder than the shouts of the oppressors who claim it's all *her* fault.

10

IT'S NOT HER FAULT

Influential men in Christian history have constructed a doctrine that claims Eve was the root cause of the fall and a source
of evil in the world. Monastic fathers believed women's bodies
were correlated with the flesh and men with the spirit,[1] and
"every act of intercourse was seen as the spirit (man) becoming
entrapped in sinful flesh (woman) and women were viewed as
insatiable and innate temptresses."[2] The early church father
Tertullian said of women, "You are the devil's gateway. . . . How
easily you destroyed man, the image of God. Because of the
death which you brought upon us, even the Son of God had to
die."[3] An androcentric analysis of the fall led early theologians
to widely accept that women are somehow "less" than men,
since the first woman came from Adam's rib, and therefore
are designated to help and serve men, in addition to their
sinfulness as the responsible party for the fall of humankind.

A patriarchal exegesis of Genesis 3:16 assumes men ought to
rule over women since God decreed to Eve, "[your husband]
will rule over you." Scholar Philip B. Payne notes that Genesis
3:16 is "God's statement of what will result from the fall, not

God's decree of what should be. Like every other result of the fall, this is something new, not in the original creation. It is a distortion of God's design." Payne adds, "Since man's ruling over woman—even good rule—is a result of the fall, man must not have ruled over woman before the fall. Furthermore, Christ, the promised seed of the woman, has overcome the fall (Gen. 3:15; 1 Cor. 15:45). New creatures freed by Christ should not foster any of the tragic consequences the fall introduced, including man's rule over woman."[4]

An egalitarian view examines Genesis 3:16 as a tragedy for both sexes. Brokenness mars the woman as she vulnerably seeks for her needs to be met by man. In his own brokenness, man dominates her, "a tragedy played out with sickening regularity throughout history," author Lucy Peppiatt notes.[5] For millennia, men, in one fashion or another, have branded women's bodies as inferior and lecherous, to be ruled. The impact of a longstanding shameful sexual ethic repackaged in purity rallies, pledges, and promise rings in the twenty-first century can be seen in the lives of women struggling to decipher their role and responsibility in matters of sexual misconduct. But the onus should not be placed on women to control the behavior of men.

If we are to care for women who've endured sexual misconduct, it will take a radical shift away from shameful theology that believes women are second, when in fact they are created with equal worth and dignity to share in authority over the earth (Gen. 1:26–28). And their bodies, however they are dressed—in leggings, spaghetti straps, or even a crop top—are not a stumbling block that will destroy men's pursuit of holiness or serve as invitation for assault. We must shatter the myth that a victim's wardrobe played a role, even a minor one, in her harassment or assault with the truth, that it's not an exterior variable that causes men to harass or assault—it is their own sinfulness that drives their actions. This starts with how we speak to our daughters: explaining that their bodies are neither a weapon nor a curse but a gift to be celebrated and respected.

In Mark 7, Jesus tells the disciples, "What comes out of a person is what defiles him. For from within, out of the heart of man, come evil thoughts, sexual immorality, theft, murder, adultery, coveting, wickedness, deceit, sensuality, envy, slander, pride, foolishness. All these evil things come from within, and they defile a person" (vv. 20–23 ESV). Our cultural tendency is to excuse men from addressing their immoral thoughts, but Jesus is clear on matters of liability: "There is nothing outside a person that by going into him can defile him, but the things that come out of a person are what defile him" (v. 15 ESV).

Men are responsible for their own actions. They are charged with patrolling their own thoughts, desires, and impulses. The misconception that men's natural disposition causes quench-less sexual desire consequently leading to harassment or assault of women only preserves the belief that women exist for the pleasure of men and are the reason for men's downfall, and unsurprisingly, it builds empathy for perpetrators.

Before victim blaming is an issue, which has more to do with the hearts of men than the appearance or actions of women, we can raise boys to think differently about women. Caregivers, counselors, and clergy addressing boys have the responsibility of addressing myths about female bodies and agency. Arming boys with a basic grasp of equality *before* they are faced with the opportunity to treat women and girls as inferior is crucial to preventing sexual misconduct. Just as rules in adulthood are shaped by culture, geography, and media, values embodied in childhood as a result of proactive caregiving, research claims, have a direct impact on how children treat others.[6]

Alison Cashin, director of the Making Caring Common project at the Harvard Graduate School of Education, ex-plains, "The most effective way for parents to insulate their sons from sexual assault allegations is to help them develop a clear understanding of assault and consent, raise them to care for and value the humanity in others, and give them the tools to work through the powerful negative emotions that can sometimes drive boys and young men in particular to violate others. In other words, there's no silver bullet. It's the hard work of parenting."[7] Cashin implies that boys are never too young to learn of the dignity beholden in others and their personal responsibility to contribute to a safe, respectable, and equal world. In short, challenge the predominant benchmarks of masculinity.

To start, caregivers can raise mindful men by properly addressing body parts and offer an age-appropriate understanding of consent with language they can understand and use. They can clearly and regularly communicate that no one has the right to touch or speak of their body parts and that they have no right to speak about or touch others' body parts without consent. No forced hugs, high-fives, or handshakes. A disregard for consent in children often manifests in bullying—aggressive speech and unwanted physical contact—which young boys may not experience at home but witness on the playground, on sports teams, in video games, in internet videos, in cartoons, from neighborhood kids, and so on. Bullying in the form of harassment ramps up in adolescence, where most girls who have been harassed in adolescence are harassed before they leave middle school.[8] During the 2010–11 school year, a study conducted by the American Association of University Women revealed that 56 percent of female students in grades 7–12 experienced sexual harassment (in person or online) in a single year.[9] Boys cave to peer pressure and harass girls to establish dominance for fear that they may appear weak to other boys *and* girls.

As boys grow up, the burden of proving they are men leads to sexist comments and harassment—physical, sexual, and verbal. Science journalist Melinda Wenner Moyer notes that "compared with other teen boys, those who endorse strong gender stereotypes—for instance, that it's natural for boys to want to admire girls and that girls should use their looks and bodies to attract men—are more likely to make sexual comments about and grab girls' bodies. This is in part because during the teen years, male gender stereotypes start to incorporate ideals of male dominance, aggression and sexual callousness, while female ideals start to center on sexuality and attractiveness."[10] With that knowledge, we should never allow our intentional conversations with adolescent boys around sex and sexuality to be reduced to preventing pregnancy and STDs, or even saving one's body for marriage, but we should include how their life choices—verbal and nonverbal communications, actions both in person and online—can prevent sexism and sexual misconduct as they honor a woman's dignity and inherent worth. Caregivers, together with the adolescent boys in their lives, can develop responses for how they will combat "locker room" banter, in person and online, to resist the macho masculinity that undergirds patriarchal culture. At every milestone, caregivers can clarify criteria for a healthy relationship versus an unhealthy relationship between boys and the opposite sex.

As we address sexism with boys, we ought to discern that chivalry is nice, but kindness is better. The traditional notion of chivalry enforces what psychologist Peter Glick of Lawrence University calls benevolent sexism—the idea that women should be cherished and put on pedestals, subtly presuming women are fragile and less competent. Glick argues that benevolent sexism "reinforces a sexual script in which a man takes charge while a woman remains passive."[11] Opening doors, picking up the tab, and "protecting" women and girls cannot come at the cost of believing girls are inferior. Kindness for kindness' sake values equality and does not assume superiority.

Experts agree that raising empathetic boys who are gracious with themselves and others requires engaging emotions as they arise. When boys are emasculated for expressing emotion with comments such as "act like a man," "toughen up," or "stop crying like a girl," research suggests they are more likely to grow up to perpetuate sexual violence.[12] Reinforcing gender stereotypes that cast boys as detached and physical and girls as helpless and emotional assumes one sex has power and the other doesn't. Furthermore, it suppresses the emotional growth necessary to acknowledge how others feel. Boys' emotions deserve validation. We must heed the words of the late Mr. Rogers, who said during a Senate hearing, "Feelings are mentionable and manageable."[13] Acknowledging feelings without punishment allows for boys to experience the emotional freedom necessary to thrive in connection with others.

When we teach boys personal responsibility, mindful masculinity, and verbal, physical, and sexual boundaries, we create a culture that doesn't assume women are responsible for what happens to them but instead creates space for everyone to be seen, heard, and cared for. No blame required.

Misplaced Empathy

As the #MeToo movement has uncovered the rampant nature of victim blaming, one study explains the influence of empathy for female victims and male perpetrators. Reported in the journal *Psychology of Women Quarterly*, a two-part study conducted with university students found that a majority of university men offered more empathy for male perpetrators and less empathy for female victims in response to a vignette describing sexual harassment. In the second half of the study, students were asked to take the perspective of either the male perpetrator or female victim, and the study revealed that "regardless of participant gender, participants who took the male-perpetrator's perspective versus the female-victim's perspective reported greater victim blame, and this was explained by their greater empathy for the male perpetrator and lesser empathy for the female victim."[14] According to this study, perpetrators can garner empathy from everybody, male or female, leaving little for the victims when they appeal to the public. This is what Cornell philosophy professor Kate Manne calls "himpathy—an excessive sympathy sometimes shown to male perpetrators of sexual violence in the attempt to preserve their reputation, power, or status."[15]

As of late, a hedge of himpathy and distorted denial of sexual misconduct has been extended by faith leaders to cover not only powerful men in ecclesiastical leadership who abused their power but also politicians. Many Christian leaders and everyday churchgoers have downplayed appalling sexual assault allegations by women against Donald Trump. Prior to his presidential election in 2016, Trump had been credibly accused of sexual harassment and assault by seventeen women, some of whom claimed they were as young as thirteen when they were first raped by the real estate mogul.[16] About a month before the election, the now-infamous *Access Hollywood* tape that included comments by Trump bragging to host Billy Bush about sexually assaulting women was leaked. Even still, in November 2016, Trump won the presidential race with strong support from white evangelicals and other groups traditionally known for family values. The *Access Hollywood* comments were not enough to sway many evangelical faith leaders and predominantly white, faithful churchgoers from voting for their "God-ordained-for-such-a-time-as-this" hero but instead prompted compassion and empathy for an alleged serial abuser.[17] In a follow-up piece recording the responses of faith leaders around the country, Sarah Pulliam Bailey of the *Washington Post* reported, "Robert Jeffress, senior pastor of First Baptist Church in Dallas and a member of Trump's Faith Advisory Council, said in a statement that he believes Trump is 'still the best candidate to reverse the downward spiral this nation is in.' David Brody from the Christian Broadcasting Network tweeted, 'This just in: Donald Trump is a flawed man! We ALL sin every single day. What if we had a "hot mic" around each one of us all the time?'" Another pro-Trump pastor mentioned by Bailey posted on Twitter, "I don't condone the conversation; but I don't condemn the man!"[18] An emphasis on God's plan to use a broken man led to a generous offer of empathy and compassion by shepherds charged with caring for the least among us, the vulnerable lambs—those without defense or a voice—but make no mistake, it isn't a perpetrator who needs empathy simply because we believe he will fulfill God's righteous plans for a nation; it is the silenced.

The dark side of empathy vilifies a victim while allowing the perpetrator unfounded compassion, perhaps an aftereffect of the implicit Christian attitude that women are naturally subject to men's rights to their bodies. Empathy for perpetrators robs the victimized of acknowledgment and reveals our inner thoughts and beliefs about a woman's place, value, and social standing. When we side with a victim's oppressor by way of empathy, we lose any trust or confidence she may have had in us as allies for her healing and justice. Therefore, reducing the misplaced empathy that observers award to perpetrators is as imperative as providing empathy for victims. The accused may appear in need of our empathy, but it's the powerless with whom we should train ourselves to empathize.

In my own experience, my unwarranted empathy for an abuser of power kept me silent when silence breaking was greatly needed. I didn't want to believe a good man would go beyond the social bounds of what both he and I knew were acceptable, and that line of thinking minimized my experience, and the experiences of women around me. The support you and I offer to an offender translates to a lack of understanding for the women he preys upon. Our empathy for a culprit limits support and care for the victimized, and the compassion from his supporters perpetuates a cycle of abuse.

Our belief in any man's perceived goodness should never outweigh our empathy for the oppressed, no matter how hard he tries to convince us that he is the casualty of slander or made out to be a monster. As we align our thinking and beliefs about women with how Christ engaged, respected, and elevated women, we rid ourselves of any political, financial, or societal reasoning that suggests it is a woman's fault for the misconduct she endures. As we consciously manage our compassion and invest it into the victimized, we can confidently speak up for the poor in spirit, those in need of justice and care, and defend them from the powerful that claim it's all her fault. Caring for victims of misconduct and curbing compassion for perpetrators does not suggest that perpetrators do not deserve the grace and mercy of God. We serve a merciful God, who is gracious with us, but a perpetrator's access to divine grace does not invalidate the severity and ramifications of his sins and crimes. Grace is not a free pass to abuse power, privilege, or position, and we must never treat it as such.

Just-World Hypothesis

For all of us who witness abuse of power, victim blaming can spring from our innate hope that the world is *already* just and good. A widespread belief that victims of misfortune get what's coming to them, enduring natural consequences because of how they looked, dressed, or carried themselves in the case of sexual harassment or assault, is what psychologists call the just-world theory. According to the theory, people have a strong propensity to believe that the world is already a good and ordered place where everyone gets what they deserve. As we order our lives, we innately assume that our actions will have predictable consequences. When evidence suggests that the world is not as it should be, we either restore justice or persuade ourselves to believe that nothing happened that should not have happened.[19] The pervasive belief that good things happen to good people who pull themselves up by their bootstraps, and bad things happen to bad people, plays well into the hypothesis. Making women liable for their own catastrophe is a method of avoidance—refusing to believe that something just as atrocious could destroy our own lives even if we play by the gendered rules of society.

Most of us, when we hear of sexual misconduct, attempt to make sense of why and how it happened. If a woman, on her own accord, remained in contact with a perpetrator, then we are led to believe she willingly placed herself in harm's way. Yet research reveals that it is quite common for victims to remain friendly with their perpetrators, especially if he is a professional acquaintance or intimate abuser. According to leaders at the Time's Up Foundation, "Because of the complex ways in which sexual assault and related coercion and abuse exploit power and control—and, thus, undermine victims' self-confidence and self-esteem—many victims struggle to break-off contact. In some instances, abusers may swear that it will never happen again, work to redeem themselves, and exploit their victim's natural tendency to forgive."[20] If the abuser has financial or professional power over a victim, she might maintain contact simply to avoid his wrath or revenge. We cannot assume that because she didn't act as we think we would that she is guilty of the misconduct committed against her.

Inwardly, we'd like to believe that we would never be subject to coercion by a man in power; therefore, if we are provided reasonable evidence to believe that a woman actively engaged her perpetrator and was somehow, in our mind, complicit in the act, then we preserve our view of the world by believing that we are protected from perpetrators. This is perfectly illustrated by Harvey Weinstein's defense lawyer Donna Rotunno, who, when asked by *New York Times* journalist Meghan Twohey on *The Daily* podcast if she had ever been sexually assaulted, replied, "No. . . . Because I would never put myself in that position."[21] The notion that disreputable women willingly place themselves in positions of compromise to be harassed perpetuates the belief that victims of sexual misconduct get what they deserve.

After *The Daily* episode was released, the hashtag #WhereIPutMyself came soon after, started by lawyer and activist Rachael Denhollander, who was the first to speak publicly against Larry Nassar. Denhollander asked victims to share where they had "put" themselves to be harmed. The responses were devastating: "simply being a toddler in my own home," "twelve at a movie," "asleep in my sleeping bag," "I was in a public park."[22] None of these people were asking for harm. It was never their fault. It is the harmed who lack a voice and power, not the oppressors. The book of Ecclesiastes speaks of the truth and tragedy facing powerless victims: "Again, I observed all the oppression that takes place under the sun. I saw the tears of the oppressed, with no one to comfort them. The oppressors have great power, and their victims are helpless" (Eccles. 4:1 NLT). Victims don't place themselves in the line of fire as much as we'd like to believe they do.

Throughout Judeo-Christian history, terrible things have been done in the name of God. Abram, the father of many nations, abused his power when he impregnated his wife's Egyptian slave-maid, Hagar, at his wife Sarai's insistence to fulfill what he believed was right in his eyes, at the expense of an innocent woman, to become what God had promised him he would become (Gen. 16). In ancient times, it was a consistent and acceptable practice to use slaves as surrogates. Hagar, who was at the mercy of her mistress, Sarai, was ordered to lay with Abram for the benefit of the Hebrew family. After she was, by modern definition, forcibly assaulted, she was despised by Sarai (as if she hadn't suffered enough). Hagar was merely an instrument for the human ambition of Abram and Sarai, not an active participant in the plans of God.

Examining the account of Hagar allows us to debunk the just-world theory and recognize that a young, fertile, Egyptian woman did not deserve the harm done to her, regardless of the acceptable practice of the day. Despite our belief that the world may already be good and just, bad things happen to good people, because offenders oppress victims with dominion and coercion. It is clearly not victims who use their resources, power, and privilege to dominate others. As we acknowledge this fundamental truth when it comes to matters of misconduct, we can refrain from treating a victim like a criminal, willing to perjure herself in order to destroy a powerful man.

As followers of Jesus, it is our responsibility to reject practices and customs of our day that harm women or blame them for misconduct, no matter how universally accepted those practices may be. It is not our job, in the court of public opinion, to decide if a woman asked for harassment or assault and then take it upon ourselves to punish her, in person or on the internet, because we believe she looked or acted like she wanted it, or because she maintained contact with the perpetrator. Her youth, body shape, smile, attire, and actions did not demand she be harmed.

The long-standing belief that women are creatures created to serve the interests of men and don't have rights of their own has poisoned our understanding of women's experiences and left them without a voice to tell the truth. The truth, not myths perpetuated by media and religion that muzzle women who've been harmed, must replace reductive knowledge we've held to throughout the centuries. If we don't understand why victims acted as they did in cases of misconduct, that is because the vast majority of us do not understand the nuanced effects of trauma, yet that must not limit us from pursuing a deep awareness and an expanded emotional capacity to sympathize with the hurting women among us. We all respond to trauma differently, and it is a marker of our emotional and spiritual growth to engage the dissonant reality that harm befalls innocent women who did absolutely nothing to deserve harassment or assault. We have to recognize that when power has been abused, it's not her fault, and it's our responsibility to care for her.

11

HE IS NOT INDISPENSABLE

In a remorseful tone, Pastor Andy Savage informed a Memphis congregation that twenty years ago, as a twenty-two-year-old high school pastor in Texas, he "regretfully had a sexual incident with a female high school senior in the church." Savage claimed that he had apologized to the victim and her family and moved from Texas to Tennessee. He offered an apology for the "incident" and said that he complied with church leadership at the time of the abuse, who oversaw his restitution process. Once Savage finished reading his letter of admission, which disclosed that his Memphis senior pastor knew of his past indiscretion, he received a standing ovation for his confession of misconduct after his victim, Jules Woodson, reached out to him by email.[1] As a seventeen-year-old girl, Woodson says, she was assaulted by Savage when he coerced her into oral sex. He immediately apologized and asked her to take what happened to the grave with her.[2] She didn't. She bravely told her parents and then church leaders; however, according to Woodson, church leadership echoed Savage's warning to stay quiet. Woodson claimed that Savage never reached out to her or her family after the abuse, he only asked that she stay silent in the situation, while Savage enjoyed a farewell party.[3]

Savage's momentary exoneration by way of applause was the tipping point of his defense. He later claimed his relationship with Woodson was consensual and explained it was legal in the state of Texas for a twenty-two-year-old to be sexually active with a seventeen-year-old. But in doing so, he ignored not only his own sexual sin but also the indisputable abuse of power that he as a youth pastor exerted over a student in the youth group.[4] His employer, Highpoint Church, did not initially terminate his employment after he confessed to the congregation; church leaders maintained Savage's defense until Woodson's story of abuse made national news. After public pressure, Savage stepped down from his position as teaching pastor at Highpoint with a letter of acknowledgment citing his abuse of a minor and ignorance on the effects of trauma.[5]

Before he publicly confessed, Savage's Texas and Tennessee congregations had no knowledge that they had a man unsuitable for ministry—based on the qualifications outlined in Titus 1:5–9; 1 Timothy 3:1–7; and 1 Peter 5:1–4—preaching from the pulpit. Disturbingly, Savage was well known for broaching taboo subjects like dating, marriage, and sex in his sermons and on his blog, even earning the nickname Sex Pastor, despite leadership at *both* congregations having knowledge of his indiscretion. Only when his victim raised her voice did the truth become public—and the public did not hesitate to respond. An online petition calling for Savage's resignation garnered 7,530 supporters.[6] A nationwide victim's rights group appealed to Savage to relinquish his position.[7] Highpoint's senior pastor resigned,[8] the Texas pastor whom Woodson told of her abuse was placed on leave and then resigned from his position,[9] and the trending hashtag #JusticeForJules called for justice and reform in the church as it handles sexual misconduct. While Woodson deserved due process and compassionate care at the time of the abuse, when faithful men and women heard of the injustice, albeit twenty years later, they spoke up.

In situations where a man is guilty of harming a woman, the question then becomes not, Did he engage in misconduct? or, Was it her fault? but, What are the consequences for his sins and/or crimes? What long-term financial, legal, and societal ramifications should he face? Could his earnest acknowledgment of abuse minimize the repercussions he is owed? If he publicly repents, is he off the hook? If he continues to deny allegations despite credible evidence, do we allow him to use his money and power to stay in his position? If he rides off into the sunset and removes his physical and digital footprint, do we let it go? Because the perpetrator's outcome is largely dependent on how others—employers, human resource departments, supporters, clergy, criminal systems, victim's advocates, journalists, protestors, and even churchgoers—perceive his actions, their individual and collective critique speaks volumes about the nature of justice, who deserves it, and who does not.

Stanford University swimmer Brock Turner faced charges after he sexually assaulted an unconscious woman on campus. In articles around the country, his accolades preceded his name. What he had accomplished, and what he could have mastered in the future, was presented as credible reasons to reduce the severity of his consequences. Turner's father went so far as to personally write the judge a letter that was read aloud at his son's sentencing hearing, explaining what he thought was best for his son, and how Brock shouldn't be punished for a mere twenty minutes of foul play out of his twenty-plus years of life.[10] Hard time wouldn't look good on him, and supposedly that was reason enough to minimize his sentence, according to Judge Aaron Persky, who reasoned that "a prison sentence would have 'a severe impact' and 'adverse collateral consequences' on Turner."[11]

In the end, Turner was sentenced to six months in the county jail and three years of probation for three felony counts of sexual assault. After three months of jail time, Turner was released. His lenient sentence was disturbing for his victim, Chanel Miller, who wrote in response to his sentencing, "How fast Brock swims does not lessen the severity of what happened to me, and should not lessen the severity of his punishment."[12] The plea for minimized consequences negated the weight of his actions against the woman he harmed.

Lenient consequences awarded to perpetrators who possess more social, racial, or financial power than their victims underscore that no matter what a perpetrator has done, if he has the ability to escape severe consequences, he will likely do just that. In recent times, this has been seen in corporate America by executives awarded significant payouts after they've been found guilty of sexual misconduct—executives like Andy Rubin, creator of the Google Android mobile software. After a Google employee reported that Rubin coerced her into oral sex, Google investigated the claim and concluded that her claim was true.[13] Rubin was asked to resign. Upon his departure, he was sent with well-wishes and a $90 million exit package to be paid in $2 million monthly installments.[14] Although Google wisely parted ways with Rubin, their initial failure to expose his actions to the company and his pricey farewell proves to sexual misconduct victims everywhere that although what happened to them was unfortunate, the well-being of the powerful is perhaps of greater importance than the consequences they are due.

Like corporate America, the church's commitment to preserving seats of power is of upmost importance, particularly in cases of sexual misconduct. As perpetrators escape consequences for their wrongdoing, many falsely assume that it would hurt the church at large to go public, that it would hurt "the witness," which translated means that it would look bad for the church if the public knew of what we, as a nonprofit religious institution, internally faced, and so it was in everyone's best interest to turn the other cheek. Evidently, Jesus needs PR, and it's up to the church to fill the job.

Justice, Justice Shall You Pursue

Correcting a broken system requires identifying and rectifying the conditions in which the abuse took place and removing the perpetrator and his enablers. To analyze conditions of the system requires those within the system receive retaliation-free opportunities to share their experiences with unbiased investigators who are trained to pinpoint dynamics and patterns of abuse. Anonymity or promise of protection should be awarded to all who come forward to share of misconduct in order to safeguard their story and reputation. Allowing *all* those impacted by the perpetrator to confide their experience is necessary; if not, key witnesses may be left out in the fact-finding process. We must not limit our investigations to poorly run internal interrogations managed by those whose primary interest is the reputation of the organization. We must commit ourselves to external, unbiased forms of investigation to discover the full truth and hold our organizations and workplaces accountable. We must commit to uncovering the truth at all costs, however buried it may be.

In most instances of allegations of misconduct, it's wise to place the alleged perpetrator on a leave of absence while his actions are investigated. In addition, the perpetrator should have no sway in the process of the investigation and should be approached only after witnesses have been interviewed. If the perpetrator is found guilty of misconduct, all impacted—employees, investors, church members, and other stakeholders—deserve transparent communication detailing the misconduct committed by the perpetrator (while protection of the victim[s] is still maintained) as well as pertinent information regarding his dismissal and steps the institution is taking to rectify the situation. If he committed a crime, authorities should be notified, and relevant parties should be encouraged by the institution to seek retribution in court, with their full support. As active enablers are identified, they too should be dismissed from their roles in an effort to rebuild trust between stakeholders and the system. Without actions such as these, it is impossible to change a permissive culture that allows women to be harassed or assaulted and then silenced.

If the misconduct committed was by a church leader, adhering to church discipline that removes the perpetrator from his position, strips him of his title, and prohibits him from gospel ministry within the denomination, as well as contacting governing authorities if the law was broken, cannot be overlooked. Church members should be notified of the proven misconduct, and opportunity for others to come forward with their experiences is necessary to grasp the full impact of abuse and to ensure all those who have been harmed are awarded care for their healing journey. For the benefit of the church at large, the matter must be handled with the utmost care and concern if the church desires to be a safe haven for the vulnerable.

Developing trauma-informed protocols in order to eradicate a permissive culture requires regular institution-wide training by experts versed in unconscious bias and gender-based harassment and assault. It requires an understanding of power dynamics and communication of clear boundaries that are universally understood by all those within the system. If boundaries are crossed, appropriate consequences should be in place for culprits—even at the highest levels—and a path of care available for victims.

For anyone in leadership, there must be limits around their power and an unbiased outsider or firm charged with assessing the health of the leadership to ensure that those subject to the leader or leadership team are not under authoritarian rule but rather a democracy where all are entitled a voice. If an employee or church member comes forward with allegations, they must be informed that their voice matters, their allegations will be heard and investigated, and they will be supported.

We must flip on every light switch, search every corner, and honestly examine the wreckage a perpetrator has left in his wake. We cannot assume the issue will go away on its own. It never has, and it never will. That's not how misconduct works. It will continue to permeate every space and infect every system until we tell the truth, until we listen to the silenced, until we offer compassion, and until we choose justice and reform.

Holding perpetrators and the system that enabled them accountable when there is testimony (or, in many cases, testimonies) of misconduct is absolutely, without exception, mandatory to protect women and uphold their dignity and inherent value as image bearers of God. Psalm 82:3–4 says, "*Give* justice to the weak and the fatherless; *maintain the right* of the afflicted and the destitute. *Rescue* the weak and the needy; *deliver* them from the hand of the wicked" (ESV, emphasis added). From this instruction we can see our active role as those coming alongside the harmed: give justice, maintain rights, rescue, and deliver. Justice for the vulnerable is not an isolated episode; it addresses the system of compromise in which she was harmed. We do ourselves a disservice when we assume that dismissing a sole perpetrator from his position and offering redress for the victim corrects the fundamental issues of control, coercion, and abuse within the structure. Comprehensive justice requires a complete overhaul of the system. If it can't be fixed, burn it until only the gold remains. How else will the #MeToo movement effect lasting change if we don't assess what's broken and right our cultural wrongs, if we don't hold the guilty parties responsible for their actions and burn down the structures that foster abuses of power?

Justice addresses the indispensable position men hold in authoritarian systems—corporations, Hollywood, sports teams, churches, educational institutions, governmental organizations, the military—and levels them as equals with others. Justice necessitates the permanent removal of a perpetrator and his coconspirators from power. Justice demands appropriate consequences assigned to the perpetrator and vindication for the victimized. Justice restores, as much as humanly possible, what's been stolen, broken, or destroyed. Justice roots out men and women guilty of enabling a perpetrator. Justice examines and reconstructs procedures, payouts, and policies that enable predators and silence women for the benefit of the perpetrator. Justice enacts laws that protect women who've been harmed and will protect potential victims in the future. Justice reorients the way of empire toward the way of the kingdom of God, where the oppressed are defended and the safety of the vulnerable is upheld in order for all God's children to thrive.

One Voice

It's not insolence to stand against the powerful people who gave you a position, a platform, or a paycheck when you defend victimized women. I intimately understand how agonizing it is to feel compelled to speak up yet be working against the ingrained belief that a quiet spirit is indicative of righteousness and there is legitimate fear of losing right standing in the community. And, for many of us with conflicting thoughts on what we should do, we quietly hope others will persist and take a bold stand so we don't have to. But we are implicated if we know of harm and do nothing.

Perhaps you may assume that you are excused from the call of justice since you have little power to exercise on behalf of women who've been silenced, slandered, or ignored. You have a voice, but it's not one of influence. Yet one voice, one singular voice, however powerful it is or isn't, raised on behalf of injustice can make way for deliverance, healing, and justice.

The voice of Moses demanded freedom for the Israelites from Pharaoh.

The voice of Daniel defied King Nebuchadnezzar as Daniel and his friends were in captivity.

The voice of Esther divulged the murderous plans of Haman to King Xerxes in an effort to save the Jewish people.

Believe me when I say there is no joy in going first—standing for truth and justice when others have yet to step up. However, whoever goes first has the honor of inviting others to speak truth, even when they feel they have nominal agency. As more women and men speak up on behalf of the silenced, the more women will be heard, acknowledged, and offered recompense for their losses, and the more systems will be forced to correct antiquated practices that oppress those who have been silenced. With strength in numbers, we can stand as a collective voice that won't be silenced no matter how hard the powerful try to shut us up.

If history shows us anything, it's that we can't expect the powerful to toe the line toward equality. More often than not, it is the oppressed and their allies who bend the arc of history toward justice.

For Chanel Miller, the lenient consequences for her rapist, Brock Turner—six months of jail time rather than the potential fourteen-year prison sentence—did not go unnoticed. Michele Dauber, a law professor at Stanford and friend of Miller, led a recall campaign backed by prominent women such as Anita Hill and Kirsten Gillibrand to remove Judge Aaron Persky from the bench. Sixty percent of voters in Santa Clara County used their vote to recall Persky from his post, thus communicating that leniency for perpetrators would not be tolerated. Persky was removed, the first judge recalled in California in over eighty years. Dauber said in a statement, "We voted that sexual violence, including campus sexual violence, must be taken seriously by our elected officials, and by the justice system." The sentencing and the consequent resistance led California lawmakers to adjust the law, enacting mandatory minimum sentences in sexual assault cases.[15]

Prompting a nationwide conversation on leniency for perpetrators of sexual misconduct, portions of Miller's 7,200-word victim impact statement were read aloud on the floor of the House of Representatives by a bipartisan group of lawmakers, eighteen in all, both men and women, to expose a broken system that desperately needs nationwide attention and rectification. Jackie Speier, the California congresswoman who organized the reading, claimed, "Reading the letter in its entirety on the House floor was an attempt to share the voice of sexual assault victims and to build support for legislation that would require the Department of Education to provide a list of institutions under investigation for sexual assault."[16] The rally cry that arose from Miller's devastating experience pushed those in power to consider others who had been silenced on campuses across the nation.

The men and women employed by Google didn't wait for justice to come from the top down. Marches protesting mismanagement of sexual harassment allegations were organized in New York City, Dublin, Silicon Valley, Singapore, Hyderabad, Berlin, Zurich, London, Chicago, and Seattle after employees discovered the payouts made to executives from a news article instead of from leaders at the company. With indignation and power in numbers, Google employees made no effort to hide their disgrace for their employer. One sign at a march read, "What do I do at Google? I work hard every day so the company can afford $90,000,000 payouts to execs who sexually harass my coworkers." The *New York Times* reported, "The organizers also produced a list of demands for changing how Google handles sexual harassment, including ending its use of private arbitration in such cases. They also asked for the publication of a transparency report on instances of sexual harassment, further disclosures of salaries and compensation, an employee representative on the company board, and a chief diversity officer who could speak directly to the board."[17] Google executives apologized for their actions, admitted that another forty-eight employees had been fired for sexual harassment, and commended the protestors and promised to take steps toward addressing the issues.[18] The poor practice wouldn't be fixed overnight, but Google had been caught by its own employees, who planned to hold Google accountable for their actions.

To aid women who have been harmed and subsequently silenced, we can speak up for them by pushing for their perpetrators to face consequences not only with human resources, denominational leaders, or bosses but also, when applicable, with law enforcement. Pursuing criminal charges when applicable is not vindictive—it is justice. In addition, we can demand the leaders of whatever system we find ourselves in to develop trauma-informed protocols to protect and care for victims when they share allegations of abuse, operating with transparency and compassion. We can use our vote to ensure women are protected with reform that defends their bodies, employment, and social standing from predatory behavior. We can hold space in our churches for the harmed to be heard and offer resources for their healing. When women are silenced after misconduct, we can all consider ourselves mandatory reporters, standing as allies to the downtrodden and poor in spirit, for they are the blessed ones to receive the kingdom of heaven (Matt. 5:3).

Every single one of us has the license and authority to speak up. Nonetheless, sometimes even when we find the courage to speak up, it may seem as though it was a waste and the losses far outweigh the gains. We may put our reputation and position on the line to speak up and lose our footing in our work, social, and faith communities. People we once loved may become strangers, and places that held so many fond memories may become but a distant memory. But in the end, we can one day stand before the throne of God knowing we have done what he asked of us: act justly, love mercy, and walk humbly with him (Mic. 6:8).

12

BELIEVE WOMEN

On a busy morning, I rushed out the door to drop my son off at preschool and made the quick five-minute walk from his school to the tiny indie coffee shop that I affectionately call my office. With one arm squeezing my laptop against my body, I awkwardly fished my credit card out of my wallet to pay for my cappuccino. As I dropped my wallet back in my bag, I caught his eye. Standing just two paces behind me, there he was, the man I made it my life's work to avoid. This time, I did not have the luxury of spotting him from behind the tinted windows of my car as he crossed the street. This time, he found me, and I wasn't going anywhere.

A year before, I would have froze.

A year before, I would have hoped for the rapture.

A year before, it would have taken me days to recover.

But in that moment, I smiled.

I smiled because I no longer sat in silence.

I smiled because I was no longer bathed in shame.

I smiled because I no longer allowed myself to feel inferior to him.

I smiled because I was believed.

As a woman, to be believed is to exhale. No longer holding your breath in hopes that someone will recognize your traumatic story for what it is: the unpopular truth. To be believed is to be seen and heard. To be acknowledged and understood. Women throughout the centuries have longed for their identities, stories, and voices to be believed. To be honored. Since the unfolding of history, God has asked us to listen to the voices of women. We must not miss our moment.

Scripture exemplifies the importance and necessity of believing women as it has radically altered individual lives, like that of Naaman, a respected army commander who believes his wife's young Israelite slave girl, who tells him he should visit the prophet in Samaria to find healing from his leprosy, and indeed he finds the relief he's longed for when he does what the little girl has proposed (2 Kings 5:1–19). Believing women changes not only individual lives but also the course of history for an entire people group. In the book of Esther, a Jewish teen who becomes queen of an ancient empire is believed by her king when she confesses that his chief counsel has planned to annihilate her people. Because she is believed, she saves an entire race from mass genocide (Esther 7). Later, in the first century, Jesus defied the judicial, civil, and religious practices that treated women as second in society. To him, they were equals with men, and their voice held weight. His actions challenged the cultural position that women's testimonies were untrustworthy, despite the common beliefs of his time. The first-century Jewish historian Flavius Josephus chronicles in his work *Antiquities of the Jews* why women should not be believed: "But let not the testimony of women be admitted, on account of the levity and boldness of their sex . . . since it is probable that they may not speak truth, either out of hope of gain, or fear of punishment."[1]

In ancient times, women were seen as incapable of truth telling, supposedly driven by advantage or terror, which is why it is all the more powerful that Jesus chose women to share news of the resurrection at a time when women's testimonies held no credence (Matt. 28:8–10; John 20:11–18). It was the woman at the well who spoke of Jesus's intimate knowledge to her townspeople and they believed her. Her testimony led others to the Messiah (John 4:28–30, 39–42). It was Mary Magdalene, not Peter or John, who was the first to report of the resurrection (John 20:18), and the circulation of that very good news hinged on believing her, a woman who had been tormented by demons and delivered by Jesus, a woman who sacrificed her life and bank account to further the ministry of her Savior (Luke 8:2–3). You and I in this modern day are invited to believe women—offering fairness and justice without discounting their voices—as they tell the truth. Although the truth might be at odds with our preconceived ideas or beliefs, when we listen, we heed the example of Jesus to treat women as worthy of dignity.

Jessica Valenti, in her book *Believe Me*, addresses the contention around believing women; she writes, "There's a reason that the most resounding and viral motto of the modern anti-sexual violence movement is 'Believe women.' It's the recognition that underneath the policy debates, anti-violence laws, and cultural progress, the foundational shift that needs to happen is simple but radical trust in women. That listening to women and bearing witness to their experiences—and having faith in their stories—could be the antidote to the American default of men's word trumping all else."[2] Trust in women does not ask that we believe all women when there is clear, contradictory proof otherwise. Rather, the plea for us to "believe women" is an appeal for equality and justice. Writer Mischa Haider further explains, "#MeToo is currently unfairly portrayed to be against due process. It is not—it instead attempts to acknowledge the anger and frustration at how long due process and justice have been denied to women both institutionally and culturally."[3] The not-so-novel idea to believe women resists the feminine trope of women as scheming liars and men as innocent. It invites unbiased investigation, testimonies of both the accuser(s) and the accused, and measured penalties for those found guilty.

What comes from believing women is not abuse of testimony but justice. For Harvey Weinstein, belief in women's testimonies came with a twenty-three-year prison sentence after a jury found him guilty of rape and committing a criminal sex act.[4] The landmark case, which proved to the world that when you speak truth to power you deserve to be heard, is proof that legal recourse and restitution is possible despite the prevalent nature of silencing women after sexual misconduct. The powerful of this world must and *can* be held accountable.

After Lifetime aired *Surviving R. Kelly,* an exposé on victims who had been coerced and abused by R&B artist Robert Kelly, women were finally believed, and months after the show aired, Kelly was charged with ten counts of aggravated criminal sexual abuse in Illinois, and later he faced federal charges for his production of child pornography and conspiracy to obstruct justice, among other charges, in New York and Chicago.[5] A cable television network known for original movies geared toward middle-aged woman believed victims who'd been silenced when those who witnessed Kelly's abuse of power turned their backs. Lifetime's broadcast was not a bid to bring down an icon but rather an act of truth telling that caught the attention of 26.8 million people.[6]

Believing women allowed brave survivors to testify against their abuser Larry Nassar in a multiday court hearing in January 2018, when he was sentenced to 175 years in prison for sexual abuse spanning over three decades. Years of innocence had been stolen, but together, women who'd been harmed by Nassar demanded restitution from Michigan State to the tune of $500 million—the largest payout by a state university in American history. When we believe women, perpetrators and the institutions that housed them owe the victimized parties restitution and redress for incalculable harm.

After seven hundred sexual abuse victims spoke out against their Southern Baptist pastors, reporting violations that spanned over twenty years,[7] the Southern Baptist Convention moved to create a Credentials Committee that tracks pastoral predators and will expel faith houses that harbor them.[8] Victims did not back down when proposed reform was initially dismissed; they kept pushing. They kept fighting.

In the 1990s, surveys show, 65 to 79 percent of women serving in the US Armed Forces were victims of harassment. The military responded by employing regular anti-harassment language, widespread education, orderly and casual reporting methods, and standardized reviews. Harassment decreased until an uptick in 2018, with service women ages seventeen to twenty-four at high risk to be violated. In response, the Defense Department announced that sexual harassment within the Armed Forces would be a criminal offense.[9]

Through every generation, as gains have been made, women have courageously broken the silence as they recognize their voice matters and they deserve protection. Baby boomers, who came of age in a time when unchecked power was prevalent and there was no legal recourse women could take, make up only 19 percent of harassment claims in the workplace, whereas generation X and millennial women each make up around 40 percent of harassment claims (according to a National Women's Law Center report covering Equal Employment Opportunity Commission [EEOC] claims from 2012 to 2016).[10] As women gain protections, social and legal language to describe their experiences, and systems that do not tolerate misconduct, they are empowered to speak of their injustices with a hope that they will be believed and valued.

Believing women is key to fighting gender-based harassment and assault. We often wait for several victims to come forward with allegations against a man before we'll take a sole woman's testimony seriously, which only downplays and dismisses her individual loss. She is more likely to be berated than believed for what she shares. But what if one woman's word held as much weight as the word of one man with power and money? What if one woman's testimony and corroboration of her story could be enough to stop an offender from preying on unsuspecting victims? What if we believed rather than silenced women when they shared with us heinous stories of misconduct? We can listen. We can learn of her story without fear that she'll ruin our own.

Throughout history we've listened to powerful men tell their story from their point of view, and we would do right to listen to every woman with a truth to tell, for men have never been wanting for a voice that determines the outcome of history or her story. Some assume that if we believe women, then we recklessly award them excessive power. Yet Jesus actively addressed the power imbalance between men and women when he treated women as equals with a voice that deserved to be heard. To assume women could easily threaten whomever they please with their erroneous reports and to falsely label the victimized as the aggressors is unfounded. As mentioned earlier, the rates of false accusations are extremely low. That is, however, what we as society have allowed men to do for eons: threaten women that report abuse, paint women as attackers, and claim crazy women are out to get them. Portraying women, especially poor, minority, or immigrant women, as powerful sparks fear in those who are convinced that women, if believed, would abuse the privilege, but any woman who risks everything to come forward with the truth does not hold more power than her abuser. It was her power and agency that was stolen. She is the victim, not the aggressor. As women tell their story, as witnesses corroborate her story, and as evidence proves her testimony, it restores power back to its rightful place when she is believed.

Believing women restores what's been broken and lost—their voice, their standing as equals—and sets in motion justice, not only for the women in question, but for all humanity. Everyone is affected when women are silenced. And every one of us has a role to play to ensure women are given a voice to speak up. As followers of Jesus, may we never allow gender, political affiliation, misunderstanding of abuse, or incorrect ideas concerning Eve and womankind to dissuade us from believing that women are worthy of a dignified voice, just as men are.

Quite honestly, when women have a voice and hold power, the world will not suffer; it will benefit. If the factors that make a system prone to abuse of power are a hierarchal structure, a male-dominated environment, and a climate that tolerates transgressions—particularly when they are committed by those in power[11]—then let's pass the torch. Research shows that it's not simply training programs or reporting systems that will end harassment, it's also hiring and promoting women. If women hold positions of power, not as a single token seat but as a practice in every sphere of society, we right the cultural wrong of female oppression. As the late Supreme Court Justice Ruth Bader Ginsburg famously said, "Women belong in all places where decisions are being made. It shouldn't be that women are the exception."[12] When women are included in urban planning, safer cities are designed.[13] When women are elected to boards, male CEOs are less overconfident and make better choices for their companies.[14] When women are empowered to work, economies flourish.[15] Experts suggest that advancing a woman's place in public, private, and social sectors could increase the global GDP by $12 trillion as early as 2025.[16]

After Anita Hill's testimony on Capitol Hill in 1991, the Senate Judiciary Committee might not have stood with Hill, but thousands of men and women across America did. More women ran for office the year after the Hill Senate hearings than any other time up to that point in American history. The year 1992 was the "Year of the Woman." Like millions of women across the country, Patty Murray, then a Washington state senator, wondered how Hill would've been treated if there were women sitting on that committee of senators. After the hearings, Murray ran for the Senate. She won. In Illinois, Carol Moseley Braun won. In California, Barbara Boxer and Dianne Feinstein won.[17] As more women sat at public decision-making tables, policies that benefited women, children, and families were enacted, such as the Violence Against Women Act and the Family and Medical Leave Act.[18] Beyoncé is right when she tells us, "My persuasion can build a nation. Endless power, with our love we can devour."[19]

Restoration Is a Process

Believing women is only the start. Broken systems must own the harm they've allowed to happen. Not only denouncing an offender but also recognizing and repenting of the misconduct that happened on their watch and how they may have mishandled it, is essential to restoring public trust and health and also to healing the system. Updated reporting procedures and policies are absolutely necessary to ensure the safety and dignity of those subject to the system, but not without first acknowledging those crushed by it. Not without identifying the harm caused. If there is ever to be a chance of reconciliation between women who've been silenced and the system that allowed their harm, repentance must be offered. Repentance with reparations—an honest apology in addition to compensation for their emotional, financial, and societal losses sends a message to victims everywhere that the harm done to the victimized was wrong and inexcusable, and that those who have the power to make it right will do so.

Integrity requires transparency—to tell the whole truth and nothing but the truth. If the leaders charged with telling the story wind up with mud on their face, we would be wise to remember that it is a small price to pay compared to all that was stolen from the women who were silenced. For fear of harming victims, those in power often refrain from telling the specific nature of abuse and why the offender cannot be trusted. Unintentionally, they protect the reputation of the offender, not the victim, when they deny those influenced by the offender the transparency they deserve. Naysayers question the verity of ambiguous claims, and sympathizers empathize with an offender without any concrete reasons for why they shouldn't. This is why clarity is a welcome asset to handling issues of misconduct and the most notable way to build trust.

In an effort to rebuild organizational integrity, we must push for women who have been silenced to have a voice in the resolution process. This tenet of civility was demonstrated by 760 young clergywomen of the United Methodist Church when they petitioned for Rev. Donald "Bud" Heckman to be stripped of clerical credentials after the United Methodist Church allowed Heckman to retire "under complaint," which allowed him to keep his credentials and denied due process to his accusers in accordance with their Just Resolution.[20] Heckman's accusers, fifteen women in total (though only four made formal complaints through church channels, including his ex-wife), alleged that Heckman had preyed on them—then were dismissed from the process handled by the West Ohio Annual Conference of the United Methodist Church.[21] Removing the voices of women and their allies from the discipline process—legal or otherwise—does not support belief in women's testimony, nor does it uphold women as worthy of equal power, and when it counts most, women are not heard. Allowing survivors to have a seat at the table of power is the wisest move in course correcting a broken system that has a known pattern of silencing victims. Six months after Heckman's case reached a resolution, he was stripped of clerical credentials by the United Methodist Church.[22] Women spoke up, they were believed, their experiences were heard, and the offender faced their recommended and suitable consequences.

Restoration takes time and considerable investment—emotional, financial, and spiritual—to repair the far-reaching damage caused by one man who abused his power. The magnitude of his misdeeds is often felt in waves when one testimony leads to another and another after that. Every new account unleashes new allegations to investigate and subsequent waves of grief, which is precisely why restoration must be regarded as a process rather than a single event or meeting. Restoration requires repentance, transparency, integrity, reparations, reconciliation, reshuffling of power to include capable women at the highest levels, and fresh vision for the road ahead. Restoration is a process, not to be ignored or delayed, but to be embraced for the healing and wholeness of everyone involved.

Raise the Banner for the Beloved

While things don't always end in the way that you and I would hope—with an apology, repentance, restitution, or criminal charges—the truth does not change and neither has Jesus, who spoke up for women who'd been silenced. We can follow his call to care for the least among us.

The Prince of Peace comforts the broken, and so must we.

The Lion of Judah protects the afflicted, and so must we.

The Lamb of God advocates for the downtrodden, and so must we.

The Son of David defends the oppressed, and so must we.

The Light of the World dignifies the lives of women, and so must we.

The Last Adam empowers the daughters of Eve, and so must we.

As men move on after scandal, we must allow women to move beyond what's happened too. They do not deserve to be defined by the harm done to them for the rest of their lives, as they are not the sum of another's sins. They are brave overcomers. Even Matthew, as he recorded the ancestors of the Messiah, did not hide the women in Jesus's family line who had irregular sexual histories but in fact purposely listed them and tied them to the Savior of us all (Matt. 1:1–16). These women—Tamar, Rahab, Bathsheba, and Mary—were not disqualified from a significant place in history because of how their oppressors or society treated them. They were, as all women are, beloved by a holy God, deserving of dignity, protection, equality, and care.

We are nowhere near where we should be as it pertains to believing women, but we are further along than we used to be. What began as whispers from women in Scripture has become a shout throughout the centuries to believe women, to speak up on their behalf, to give them a seat of power, and to stand with them even when those who do so have something to lose. We, as people of God, can lift our cries, throw open our arms, and weep with those who've been silenced as we march with them toward the sunset of justice and mercy. As the oppressed and harmed search for safety and restoration, and as women fight to rise above systemic and gendered oppression, may our banner forever read, "Take your place at the table, sister. You are welcome here."

NOTES

Introduction

1. Some resources for those who have been affected by workplace harassment or violence are available from the Equal Employment Opportunity Commission at https://www.eeoc.gov or through https://metoomvmt.org.

2. "Sexual Harassment," RAINN, https://www.rainn.org/articles/sexual -harassment (emphasis added).

Chapter One: Everything Is Just Fine

1. Navneet Alang, "Stewed Awakening," *Eater*, May 20, 2020, http://www .eater.com/2020/5/20/21262304/global-pantry-alison-roman-bon-appetit.

2. Talia Lakritz, "11 Surprising Double Standards That Still Exist for Women in the US," *Insider*, March 8, 2020, https://www.insider.com/women -double-standards-sexism-2018-10.

3. Annette McDermott, "How World War II Empowered Women," *History*, July 2, 2018, https://www.history.com/news/how-world-war-ii-empowered -women.

4. Michelle Miller, "Sailor, Nurse from VJ Day Photo Reunited," *CBS News*, August 11, 2012, https://www.cbsnews.com/news/sailor-nurse-from-iconic-vj -day-photo-reunited.

5. Brooke L. Blower, "WWII's Most Iconic Kiss Wasn't Romantic—It Was Terrifying," *The Washington Post*, February 22, 2019, https://www.washing tonpost.com/outlook/2019/02/22/wwiis-most-iconic-kiss-wasnt-romantic -it-was-assault.

6. Kimberle Crenshaw, "Mapping the Margins: Intersectionality, Identity Politics, and Violence against Women of Color," *Stanford Law Review* 43, no. 6 (July 1991): 1241–99, https://doi.org/10.2307/1229039.

7. Amanda Rossie, Jasmine Tucker, and Kayla Patrick, "Out of the Shadows: An Analysis of Sexual Harassment Charges Filed by Working Women,"

National Women's Law Center, https://nwlc.org/wp-content/uploads/2018/08/SexualHarassmentReport.pdf.

8. Princess Daazhraii Johnson, "What's Missing from #METOO and #TIMESUP: One Indigenous Woman's Perspective," *Native Movement*, January 20, 2018, https://www.nativemovement.org/nm-blog/2018/1/20/whats-missing-from-metoo-and-timesup-one-indigenous-womans-perspective.

9. Julia Hale, "From #METOO to #TIMESUP: How Undocumented Women Fit in the Women's Movement," *Chicago Tribune*, April 24, 2018, https://www.chicagotribune.com/voice-it/ct-hoy-from-metoo-to-timesup-how-undocumented-women-fit-in-the-women-s-movement-20180424-story.html.

10. James Queally, "Latinos Are Reporting Fewer Sexual Assaults amid a Climate of Fear in Immigrant Communities, LAPD Says," *Los Angeles Times*, March 21, 2017, https://www.latimes.com/local/lanow/la-me-ln-immigrant-crime-reporting-drops-20170321-story.html.

11. Rebecca Leung and Robert Williams, "#MeToo and Intersectionality: An Examination of the #MeToo Movement through the R. Kelly Scandal," *Journal of Communication Inquiry* 43, no. 4 (October 2019): 349–71, https://doi.org/10.1177/0196859919874138.

12. Jim DeRogatis, "Inside the Pied Piper of R&B's 'Cult,'" *Buzzfeed News*, July 17, 2017, https://www.buzzfeednews.com/article/jimderogatis/parents-told-police-r-kelly-is-keeping-women-in-a-cult.

13. Leung and Williams, "#MeToo and Intersectionality."

14. Eliza Berman, "Meet the Activists Who Accompanied Celebrities on the Golden Globes Red Carpet," *Time*, January 7, 2018, https://time.com/5091772/golden-globes-red-carpet-activists.

15. Chimamanda Ngozi Adichie, *We Should All Be Feminists* (New York: Anchor Books, 2015), 13.

Chapter Two: His Way or the Highway

1. "DSM-IV and DSM-5 Criteria for the Personality Disorders," American Psychiatric Association, 2012, https://www.nyu.edu/gsas/dept/philo/courses/materials/Narc.Pers.DSM.pdf. See *Diagnostic and Statistical Manual for Mental Disorders: DSM-5*, 5th ed. (Washington, DC: American Psychiatric Association, 2013).

2. Terry Gross, "'No Visible Bruises' Upends Stereotypes of Abuse, Sheds Light on Domestic Violence," *NPR*, May 7, 2019, https://npr.org/sections/health-shots/2019/05/07/721005929/no-visible-bruises-upends-stereotypes-of-abuse-sheds-light-on-domestic-violence.

3. Heather McLaughlin, Christopher Uggen, and Amy Blackstone, "Sexual Harassment, Workplace Authority, and the Paradox of Power," *American Sociological Review* 77, no. 4 (August 2012): 625–47, https://doi.org/10.1177/0003122412451728.

4. Michelle Lee, Melanie Russo, Yana Petri, Arjun Chandran, and Cassidy Hardin, "Shifting Power Dynamics: The #MeToo Movement," *Berkeley Scientific Journal* 22, no. 2 (2018): 35–38, https://escholarship.org/uc/item/5rx2z7h9.

5. Rowena Chiu, "Harvey Weinstein Told Me He Liked Chinese Girls," *New York Times*, October 5, 2019, https://nytimes.com/2019/10/05/opinion /sunday/harvey-weinstein-rowena-chiu.html.

6. Chiu, "Harvey Weinstein Told Me He Liked Chinese Girls."

7. Shahida Arabi, *Becoming the Narcissist's Nightmare: How to Devalue and Discard the Narcissist While Supplying Yourself* (Grand Haven, MI: Audible Studios on Brilliance Audio, 2017).

8. Lindsay Dodgson, "Manipulative People Hook Their Victims with a Tactic Called 'Love Bombing'—Here Are the Signs You've Been a Target," *Business Insider*, February 6, 2018, https://businessinsider.com/what-is-love -bombing-2017-7.

9. Jada Pinkett Smith and Ramani Durvasula, "The Narcissism Epidemic," *Red Table Talk*, Facebook Watch, October 28, 2019, www.facebook.com/watch /?v=571984246943596.

10. Chuck DeGroat, "When Narcissism Comes to . . . Church Doctrine (Part 1—Introduction)," Chuck DeGroat, July 9, 2018, https://chuckdegroat .net/2018/07/08/when-narcissism-comes-to-church-doctrine-part-1-intro duction.

11. Leon F. Seltzer, "The Catch-22 of Dealing with a Narcissist," *Psychology Today*, November 1, 2017, https://psychologytoday.com/us/blog/evolution -the-self/201711/the-catch-22-dealing-narcissist.

12. Deneen L. Brown, "She Said Her Boss Raped Her in a Bank Vault. Her Sexual Harassment Case Would Make Legal History," *Washington* Post, October 13, 2017, https://www.washingtonpost.com/news/retropolis/wp /2017/10/13/she-said-her-boss-raped-her-in-a-bank-vault-her-sexual-harass ment-case-would-make-legal-history.

13. Tony Mauro, *Illustrated Great Decisions of the Supreme Court* (Washington, DC: CQ Press, 2006), 312.

Chapter Three: Be Quiet

1. A. E. Wilson, M. D. Smith, and H. R. Ross, "The Nature and Effects of Young Children's Lies," *Social Development* 12 (2003): 21–45, https://doi:10 .1111/1467-9507.00220.

2. V. Talwar and A. M. Crossman, "Children's Lies and Their Detection: Implications for Child Witness Testimony," *Developmental Review* 32, no. 4 (December 2012): 337–59, https://doi:10.1016/j.dr.2012.06.004

3. T. D. Lyon, L. C. Malloy, J. A. Quas, and V. A. Talware, "Coaching, Truth Induction, and Young Maltreated Children's False Allegations and False Denials," *Child Development* 79, no. 4 (July–August 2008), 914–29, https:// doi.org/10.1111/j.1467-8624.2008.01167.x.

4. M. L. Slepian, J. N. Kirby, and E. K. Kalokerinos, "Shame, Guilt, and Secrets on the Mind," *Emotion* 20, no. 2 (2020): 323–28, https://doi.org/10.1037 /emo0000542.

5. Michael Slepian, "Why the Secrets You Keep Are Hurting You," *Scientific American*, February 5, 2019, https://scientificamerican.com/article/why-the -secrets-you-keep-are-hurting-you.

6. David Bauder, "More Than 20 Million People Watched Kavanaugh Hearing," *AP News*, September 28, 2018, https://apnews.com/caa510f21dcd4c569 a4c8ea91f587a44/More-than-20-million-people-watched-Kavanaugh-hearing.

7. Haley Sweetland Edwards, "How Christine Blasey Ford's Testimony Changed America," *Time*, October 4, 2018, https://time.com/5415027 /christine-blasey-ford-testimony.

8. Emma Brown, "California Professor, Writer of Confidential Brett Kavanaugh Letter, Speaks Out about Her Allegation of Sexual Assault," *Washington Post*, September 16, 2018, https://www.washingtonpost.com/investigations /california-professor-writer-of-confidential-brett-kavanaugh-letter-speaks-out -about-her-allegation-of-sexual-assault/2018/09/16/46982194-b846-11e8-9 4eb-3bd52dfe917b_story.html.

9. James Hopper and David Lisak, "Why Rape and Trauma Survivors Have Fragmented and Incomplete Memories," *Time*, December 9, 2014, https:// time.com/3625414/rape-trauma-brain-memory.

10. Tim Mak, "Kavanaugh Accuser Christine Blasey Ford Continues Receiving Threats, Lawyers Say," *NPR*, November 8, 2018, https://npr.org/2018 /11/08/665407589/kavanaugh-accuser-christine-blasey-ford-continues -receiving-threats-lawyers-say.

11. Jacey Fortin, "#WhyIDidntReport: Survivors of Sexual Assault Share Their Stories after Trump Tweet," *New York Times*, September 23, 2018, https:// www.nytimes.com/2018/09/23/us/why-i-didnt-report-assault-stories.html.

12. yinaa (@czasopaqu), "#whyididntreport he told me it was my fault, and I believed him," Twitter, June 2, 2020, 9:27 p.m., https://twitter.com/czaso paqu/status/1268036546642378753.

13. #blacklivesmatter (@flyingawxy), "#whyididntreport bc he was 12 years older, he knew people I knew, he was 6ft + and I'm 5'3, I was scared he would hurt me if I did, I was scared I wouldn't be believed, I didn't even believe myself that I'd done nothing wrong. I still struggle with accepting I wasn't to blame," Twitter, June 6, 2020, 12:46 p.m., https://twitter.com/flyingawxy /status/1269354915614412800.

14. Spud (@SwilleyAngel), "Because I was 6 years old. Because he was suppose to be 'family.' Because I convinced myself for 14 years that it was a morbid dream I had when I was little," Twitter, June 5, 2020, 4:14 p.m., https://twitter.com/SwilleyAngel/status/1269045021111549953.

15. kait (@kaitlynlawson_), "i was 10, in the back of a church bus and had no idea what was happening . . . #whyididntreport," Twitter, June 5, 2020, 9:32 a.m., https://twitter.com/kaitlynlawson_/status/1268943772240547842.

16. court (@courtneyputtock), "#whyididntreport he was my mums boyfriend and she had just lost my dad after 30 years of marriage, i didn't want to hurt her or be the reason she lost someone else :/," Twitter, June 2, 2020, 1:08 p.m., https://twitter.com/courtneyputtock/status/1267910859088674822.

17. dilpreet- BLM (@dpreetx), "#whyididntreport i was 10, he told me he would hurt my mom if I did But once he did something to my sister who was 5 YEARS OLD I finally got the courage to speak up about my sister but not about myself," Twitter, June 2, 2020, 4:55 p.m., https://twitter.com /dpreetx/status/1267968095395524608.

18. Natalie Tackett (@natalie14), "#whyididntreport because people told me not to ruin his life and reputation, as if his punishment was more severe than mine. I have to live with the nightmares and anxiety while he just lives on," Twitter, June 3, 2020, 2:54 p.m., https://twitter.com/natalie14/status/1268300155020890113.

19. Diana (@dianathuytien), "#whyididntreport he knew where my entire family lived and threatened to harm them in any way possible," Twitter, June 2, 2020, 12:26 p.m., https://twitter.com/dianathuytien/status/1267900416706002944.

20. Alana Semuels, "Low-Wage Workers Aren't Getting Justice for Sexual Harassment," *The Atlantic*, December 27, 2017, https://www.theatlantic.com/business/archive/2017/12/low-wage-workers-sexual-harassment/549158.

21. "US: Sexual Violence, Harassment of Immigrant Farmworkers," Human Rights Watch, May 15, 2012, https://www.hrw.org/news/2012/05/15/us-sexual-violence-harassment-immigrant-farmworkers.

22. Orly Lobel, "NDA's Are Out of Control: Here's What Needs to Change," *Harvard Business Review*, January 30, 2018, https://hbr.org/2018/01/ndas-are-out-of-control-heres-what-needs-to-change.

23. Michelle Dean, "Contracts of Silence," *Columbia Journalism Review*, Winter 2018, https://cjr.org/special_report/nda-agreement.php.

24. Diana Falzone, "After *Catch and Kill* Fallout, Former Fox News Staffers Demand to Be Released from Their NDAs," *Vanity Fair*, October 28, 2019, https://vanityfair.com/news/2019/10/former-fox-news-staffers-demand-to-be-released-from-their-ndas.

25. Elizabeth A. Harris, "Despite #MeToo Glare, Efforts to Ban Secret Settlements Stop Short," *New York Times*, June 14, 2019, https:///nytimes.com/2019/06/14/arts/metoo-movement-nda.html.

26. Jodi Kantor and Megan Twohey, *She Said: Breaking the Sexual Harassment Story That Helped Ignite a Movement* (London: Penguin, 2019), 77.

27. Phyllis Trible, *Texts of Terror: Literary-Feminist Readings of Biblical Narratives* (Minneapolis: Fortress, 1984).

28. While this is not an immediate consolation for Tamar, we do see that Absalom doesn't follow his own advice not to worry about it, and his future is shaped by the revenge he takes on his sister's behalf.

29. Jen Wilkin, "Can We Finally Break the Silence around Tamar?" *Christianity Today*, May 17, 2019, https://christianitytoday.com/ct/2019/june/tamar-jen-wilkin-absalom-david-1-samuel.html.

Chapter Four: But He's Done So Much for Me

1. Manya Brachear Pashman and Jeff Coen, "After Years of Inquiries, Willow Creek Pastor Denies Misconduct Allegations," *Chicago Tribune*, March 23, 2018, https://www.chicagotribune.com/news/breaking/ct-met-willow-creek-pastor-20171220-story.html.

2. Jodi Kantor, "Seeing Abuse, and a Pattern too Familiar," *New York Times*, September 9, 2014, https://nytimes.com/2014/09/10/us/seeing-abuse-and-a-pattern-too-familiar.html.

3. Kantor, "Seeing Abuse."

4. Aaron Wilson, "In Wide-Ranging 'Today' Interview, Janay Rice Says Ravens Suggested She Apologize at May News Conference," *Baltimore Sun*, December 1, 2014, https://www.baltimoresun.com/sports/ravens/bal-janay -rice-discusses-her-apology-awkward-press-conference-during-today-interview -20141201-story.html.

5. James Ullrich, "Corporate Stockholm Syndrome," *Psychology Today*, March 14, 2014, https://psychologytoday.com/us/blog/the-modern-time -crunch/201403/corporate-stockholm-syndrome.

6. Eyal Winter, "Stockholm Bias: It's Not Quite Stockholm Syndrome, but It Affects All of Us," *Forbes*, August 8, 2015, https://forbes.com/sites/forbesleader shipforum/2015/04/08/stockholm-bias-its-not-quite-stockholm-syndrome -but-it-affects-all-of-us/#3e64615134e8.

7. Tim Evans, Mark Alesia, and Marisa Kwiatkowski, "Former USA Gymnastics Doctor Accused of Abuse," *Indianapolis Star*, September 12, 2016, https://indystar.com/story/news/2016/09/12/former-usa-gymnastics-doctor -accused-abuse/89995734.

8. Abigail Pesta, *The Girls: An All-American Town, a Predatory Doctor, and the Untold Story of the Gymnasts Who Brought Him Down* (New York: Seal, 2019), 120.

9. Evans, Alesia, and Kwiatkowski, "Former USA Gymnastics Doctor Accused of Abuse."

10. Pesta, *The Girls*, 64.

11. Pesta, *The Girls*, 65.

12. Megan Twohey, Jodi Kantor, Susan Dominus, Jim Rutenberg, and Steve Eder, "Weinstein's Complicity Machine," *New York Times*, December 5, 2017, https://nytimes.com/interactive/2017/12/05/us/harvey-weinstein -complicity.html.

13. Jodi Kantor and Rachel Abrams, "Gwyneth Paltrow, Angelina Jolie and Others Say Weinstein Harassed Them," *New York Times*, October 10, 2017, https://nytimes.com/2017/10/10/us/gwyneth-paltrow-angelina-jolie -harvey-weinstein.html.

14. Dennis S. Reina and Michelle L. Reina, *Trust and Betrayal in the Workplace: Building Effective Relationships in Your Organizations* (San Francisco: Berrett-Koehler, 2006), 55.

Chapter Five: What Do You Have to Lose?

1. Diana R Garland, "When Wolves Wear Shepherd's Clothing: Helping Women Survive Clergy Sexual Abuse," *Journal of Religion and Abuse* 8, no. 2 (2006): 37–70, https://doi.org/10.1300/J154v08n02_04.

2. Manya Brachear Pashman and Jeff Coen, "After Years of Inquiries, Willow Creek Pastor Denies Misconduct Allegations," *Chicago Tribune*, March 23, 2018, https://www.chicagotribune.com/news/breaking/ct-met-willow-creek -pastor-20171220-story.html.

3. Frank Newport, "Presidential Job Approval: Bill Clinton's High Ratings in the Midst of Crisis, 1998," Gallup, June 4, 1999, https://news.gallup.com /poll/4609/presidential-job-approval-bill-clintons-high-ratings-midst.aspx.

4. Todd S. Purdum, "Did Bill Clinton See This Coming?," *The Atlantic*, August 19, 2019, https://theatlantic.com/politics/archive/2019/08/bill-clinton-legacy/596323.

5. "Exclusive: Monica Lewinsky Writes about Her Affair with President Clinton," *Vanity Fair*, May 6, 2014, https://vanityfair.com/news/2014/05/monica-lewinsky-speaks.

6. Allison P. Davis, "Every Rap Song That Mentions Monica Lewinsky," *The Cut*, March 24, 2015, https://thecut.com/2015/03/every-rap-song-that-mentions-monica-lewinsky.html.

7. "Transcript: President Bill Clinton Says He's Sorry," CNN, December 11, 1998, https://cnn.com/ALLPOLITICS/stories/1998/12/11/transcripts/clinton.html.

8. "Exclusive."

9. Mark L. Egan, Gregor Matvos, and Amit Seru, "When Harry Fired Sally: The Double Standard in Punishing Misconduct" (NBER Working Paper No. 23242, National Bureau of Economic Research, March 2017), 28–29, http://www.nber.org/papers/w23242.pdf.

10. *Barriers to Justice: How the Supreme Court's Recent Rulings Will Affect Corporate Behavior*, June 29, 2011, 3, https://www.judiciary.senate.gov/imo/media/doc/11-6-29%20Dukes%20Testimony.pdf (statement of Betty Dukes, Lead Plaintiff in Walmart, Inc. v. Dukes).

11. Michele Gelfand and Virginia Choi, "The Pay Gap Is Far from the Only Discrimination Women Face," *Time*, April 2, 2019, https://time.com/5562441/equal-pay-wage-punishment-gap.

12. Frederik Obermaier and Bastian Obermayer, "Op-Ed: Whistleblowers Are Vital to Democracy. We Need to Better Protect Them," *Los Angeles Times*, April 9, 2018, https://latimes.com/opinion/op-ed/la-oe-obermaier-obermayer-whistleblowers-20180409-story.html.

13. Ronan Farrow, *Catch and Kill: Lies, Spies, and a Conspiracy to Protect Predators* (New York: Hachette, 2019), 379.

14. Roomy Khan, "Whistleblower: Warrior, Saboteur or Snitch?," *Forbes*, July 5, 2018, https://forbes.com/sites/roomykhan/2018/07/05/whistleblower-warrior-saboteur-or-snitch.

Chapter Six: The Questioning

1. Maria Cramer, "Judge Who Asked Woman If She Closed Her Legs to Prevent Assault Is Removed," *New York Times*, May 27, 2020, https://www.nytimes.com/2020/05/27/nyregion/nj-judge-john-russo.html.

2. Albert Samaha, "An 18-Year-Old Said She Was Raped while in Police Custody. The Officers Say She Consented," *Buzzfeed News*, February 27, 2018, https://www.buzzfeednews.com/article/albertsamaha/this-teenager-accused-two-on-duty-cops-of-rape-she-had-no.

3. Claire Lampen, "No Prison Time for Ex-Cops Accused of Raping Teen in Custody," *The Cut*, August 30, 2019, https://www.thecut.com/2019/08/nypd-cops-get-probation-for-having-sex-with-teen-in-custody.html.

4. Hillary McBride, email message to author, August 26, 2020.

5. "Rape Culture," Women's Center, Marshal University, https://www.mar shall.edu/wcenter/sexual-assault/rape-culture.

6. People v. Dohring, 59 N.Y. 374, 17 Am. Rep. 349, 355 (1874).

7. Reva B. Seigel, "Introduction: A Short History of Sexual Harassment," *Directions in Sexual Harassment Law* (2003): 4, https://doi.org/10.12987/yale /9780300098006.003.0001.

8. Heather McLaughlin, Christopher Uggen, and Amy Blackstone, "Sexual Harassment, Workplace Authority, and the Paradox of Power," *American Sociological Review* 77, no. 4 (2012): 625–47, https://doi.org/10.1177/000312 2412451728.

9. Shaila Dewan, "Why Women Can Take Years to Come Forward with Sexual Assault Allegations," *New York Times*, September 18, 2019, https:// www.nytimes.com/2018/09/18/us/kavanaugh-christine-blasey-ford.html.

10. Irin Carmon and Amy Brittain, "Eight Women Say Charlie Rose Sexually Harassed Them—with Nudity, Groping and Lewd Calls," *Washington Post*, November 20, 2017, https://www.washingtonpost.com/investigations/eight -women-say-charlie-rose-sexually-harassed-them–with-nudity-groping-and -lewd-calls/2017/11/20/9b168de8-caec-11e7-8321-481fd63f174d_story.html.

11. Chanel Miller, *Know My Name: A Memoir* (New York: Viking, 2019), 290–91.

12. Mark Ballenger, "3 Ways to Wrongly Apply Matthew 18," The Roys Report, February 15, 2018, https://julieroys.com/3-ways-wrongly-apply -matthew-18.

Chapter Seven: Puppets of the Patriarchy

1. Celia Swanson, "Are You Enabling a Toxic Culture without Realizing It?," *Harvard Business Review*, August 22, 2019, https://hbr.org/2019/08/are -you-enabling-a-toxic-culture-without-realizing-it.

2. Ronan Farrow, "Harvey Weinstein's Secret Settlements," *New Yorker*, November 21, 2017, https://www.newyorker.com/news/news-desk/harvey -weinsteins-secret-settlements.

3. Farrow, "Harvey Weinstein's Secret Settlements."

4. Jim DeRogatis, *Soulless: The Case against R. Kelly* (New York: Abrams, 2019), 263.

5. Christine Hauser, "Former Student Sues Harvard over Handling of Sexual Crime Complaints," *New York Times*, February 19, 2016, https://www.ny times.com/2016/02/20/us/harvard-sexual-crimes-complaints-alyssa-leader .html.

6. Jennifer Steinhauer and David S. Joachim, "55 Colleges Named in Federal Inquiry into Handling of Sexual Assault Cases," *New York Times*, May 1, 2014, https://www.nytimes.com/2014/05/02/us/politics/us-lists-colleges -under-inquiry-over-sex-assault-cases.html.

7. Brian A. Pappas, "Sexual Misconduct on Campus," *Dispute Resolution Magazine*, Winter 2019, https://www.americanbar.org/groups/dispute_resolu tion/publications/dispute_resolution_magazine/2019/winter-2019-me -too/sexual-misconduct-on-campus. See also "Dear Colleague Letter," US

Department of Education, Office for Civil Rights, September 22, 2017; and "Q&A on Campus Sexual Misconduct," US Department of Education, Office for Civil Rights, September 2017.

8. David Gelles and Claire Cain Miller, "Business Schools Now Teaching #MeToo, N.F.L. Protests and Trump," *New York Times*, December 25, 2017, https://www.nytimes.com/2017/12/25/business/mba-business-school-ethics.html.

9. Michael M. Grynbaum and John Koblin, "Gretchen Carlson of Fox News Files Harassment Suit against Roger Ailes," *New York Times*, July 6, 2016, https://www.nytimes.com/2016/07/07/business/media/gretchen-carlson-fox-news-roger-ailes-sexual-harassment-lawsuit.html.

10. Brian Flood, "Greta Van Susteren Defends Roger Ailes against Sex Harassment Claim (Exclusive)," *The Wrap*, July 7, 2016, https://www.thewrap.com/greta-van-susteren-defends-roger-ailes-gretchen-carlson.

11. Chris Ariens, "Kimberly Guilfoyle in 'Total Disbelief' about Gretchen Carlson's Sexual Harassment Suit," *Adweek*, July 10, 2016, https://www.adweek.com/tvnewser/kimberly-guilfoyle-in-total-disbelief-about-gretchen-carlsons-sexual-harassment-suit/298398.

12. Lindsey Ellefson, "EXCLUSIVE: Harris Faulkner, Martha MacCallum, and Ainsley Earhardt Speak Out on Being Women at Fox News," *Mediaite*, July 11, 2016, https://www.mediaite.com/online/exclusive-harris-faulkner-martha-maccallum-and-ainsley-earhardt-speak-out-on-being-women-at-fox-news.

13. Marisa Guthrie, "More Female Fox News Anchors Come Forward to Defend Roger Ailes," *Hollywood Reporter*, July 11, 2016, https://www.hollywoodreporter.com/news/more-female-anchors-defend-fox-909866.

14. Carol Gilligan and Naomi Snider, *Why Does Patriarchy Persist?* (Cambridge: Polity, 2018), 33.

15. Rachel Elizabeth Cargle, "When Feminism Is White Supremacy in Heels," *Harper's Bazaar*, August 16, 2018, https://www.harpersbazaar.com/culture/politics/a22717725/what-is-toxic-white-feminism.

16. "Votes for Women Means Votes for Black Women," National Women's History Museum, August 16, 2018, https://www.womenshistory.org/articles/votes-women-means-votes-black-women.

Chapter Eight: Look at Who I Am

1. Rebecca Ruiz, "People Often Defend an Alleged Rapist's Character," *Mashable*, July 24, 2016, https://mashable.com/2016/07/24/why-people-defend-men-accused-of-bad-things.

2. Tim Hindle, "The Halo Effect," *Economist*, October 14, 2009, https://www.economist.com/news/2009/10/14/the-halo-effect.

3. Richard Shweder, "What Is the Halo Effect?," *Psychology Today*, accessed January 10, 2020, https://www.psychologytoday.com/us/basics/halo-effect.

4. Patrick Healy, "Confirmation Bias: How It Affects Your Organization and How to Overcome It," *Harvard Business School Online*, August 18, 2016, https://online.hbs.edu/blog/post/confirmation-bias-how-it-affects-your-organization-and-how-to-overcome-it.

5. Lloyd Grove, "Clients Turn on 'Champion for Women' Lisa Bloom after Her Scorched-Earth Crusade for Harvey Weinstein," *The Daily Beast*, October 30, 2017, https://www.thedailybeast.com/lisa-bloom-has-files-on -rose-mcgowans-history-inside-her-scorched-earth-crusade-for-harvey-wein stein.

6. "False Reporting," National Sexual Violence Resource Center, 2012, https://www.nsvrc.org/sites/default/files/2012-03/Publications_NSVRC _Overview_False-Reporting.pdf.

7. Karen Dion, Ellen Berscheid, and Elaine Walster, "What Is Beautiful Is Good," *Journal of Personality and Social Psychology* 24, no. 3 (1972): 285–89, https://doi.org/10.1037/h0033731.

8. Melanie Mason, "California Assemblyman Accused of Forcing Lobbyist into Bathroom and Masturbating," *Los Angeles Times*, December 4, 2017, https://www.latimes.com/politics/la-pol-ca-matt-dababneh-harassment -20171204-story.html.

9. Mason, "California Assemblyman Accused of Forcing Lobbyist into Bathroom and Masturbating."

10. Jennifer J. Freyd, "What is DARVO?," University of Oregon, http:// pages.uoregon.edu/dynamic/jjf/defineDARVO.html.

11. Madison Pauly, "She Said, He Sued," *Mother Jones*, March/April 2020, https://www.motherjones.com/crime-justice/2020/02/metoo-me-too -defamation-libel-accuser-sexual-assault.

12. Lisa Lerer, "Joe Biden Jokes about Hugging in a Speech, Then Offers a Mixed Apology," *New York Times*, April 5, 2019, https://www.nytimes.com /2019/04/05/us/politics/joe-biden-controversy.html.

13. Dache Keltner, "Sex, Power, and the Systems That Enable Men Like Harvey Weinstein," *Harvard Business Review*, October 13, 2017, https://hbr.org /2017/10/sex-power-and-the-systems-that-enable-men-like-harvey-weinstein.

14. Julia Jacobs, "Anita Hill's Testimony and Other Key Moments from the Clarence Thomas Hearings," *New York Times*, September 20, 2018, https:// www.nytimes.com/2018/09/20/us/politics/anita-hill-testimony-clarence -thomas.html.

15. Victoria M. Massie, "How Racism and Sexism Shaped the Clarence Thomas/Anita Hill Hearing," *Vox*, April 16, 2016, https://www.vox.com/2016 /4/16/11408576/anita-hill-clarence-thomas-confirmation.

16. Melissa Harris-Perry, "EXCLUSIVE: Melissa Harris-Perry Interviews Anita Hill, 25 Years Later," *Essence*, March 30, 2016, https://www.essence.com /celebrity/exclusive-melissa-harris-perry-interviews-anita-hill-25-years-later.

17. Jacobs, "Anita Hill's Testimony."

Chapter Nine: Allies

1. W. Brad Johnson and David G. Smith, "How Men Can Become Better Allies to Women," *Harvard Business Review*, October 12, 2018, https://hbr.org /2018/10/how-men-can-become-better-allies-to-women.

2. Laurie A. Rudman, Kris Mescher, and Corinne A. Moss-Racusin, "Reactions to Gender Egalitarian Men: Perceived Feminization Due to Stigma-

by-Association," *Group Processes & Intergroup Relations* 16, no. 5 (September 2013): 572–99, https://doi.org/10.1177/1368430212461160.

3. Tal H. Peretz, "The Pedestal Effect: Problems and Potentiality for Feminist Men," UCLA: Center For the Study of Women, February 2008, https://escholarship.org/uc/item/1hr6f62t.

4. Susan Brownmiller, *Against Our Will* (New York: Simon & Schuster, 1975), 17.

5. Jennifer Wright, "The Decade of Enduring Male Fragility," *Harper's Bazaar*, December 27, 2019, https://www.harpersbazaar.com/culture/features/a30324982/rise-of-online-harassment-decade-of-male-fragility.

6. Jennifer Brown, "From Unaware to Accomplice: The Ally Continuum," Jennifer Brown Consulting, July 16, 2018, http://jenniferbrownconsulting.com/blog/from-unaware-to-accomplice-the-ally-continuum.

7. Tom Gjelten, "For Evangelicals, a Year of Reckoning on Sexual Sin and Support for Donald Trump," *NPR*, December 24, 2018, https://www.npr.org/2018/12/24/678390550/for-evangelicals-a-year-of-reckoning-on-sexual-sin-and-support-for-donald-trump.

8. Sharyn J. Potter and Mary M. Moynihan, "Bringing in the Bystander In-Person Prevention Program to a US Military Installation: Results from a Pilot Study," *Military Medicine* 176, no. 8 (August 2011): 870–75, https://doi.org/10.7205/MILMED-D-10-00483.

9. Claire Cain Miller, "The #MeToo Moment: How to Be a Good Bystander," *New York Times*, December 12, 2017, https://www.nytimes.com/2017/12/12/us/the-metoo-moment-how-to-be-a-good-bystander.html.

10. "#Silence Is Not Spiritual Statement," Silence Is Not Spiritual, 2019, https://silenceisnotspiritual.org/statement.

Chapter Ten: It's Not Her Fault

1. This association of women's bodies with the flesh and men's bodies with the spirit comes from an infusion of Greek philosophy into early Christianity. The monastic fathers didn't invent this idea so much as they inherited and appropriated it.

2. Lisa Isherwood and Elizabeth Stuart, *Introducing Body Theology* (Sheffield: Sheffield Academic, 1998), 18.

3. Cited in Mary Daly, *Beyond God the Father: Toward a Philosophy of Women's Liberation* (Boston: Beacon, 1973), 44.

4. Philip B. Payne, "Examining the Twelve Biblical Pillars of Male Hierarchy," CBE International, October 31, 2012, https://www.cbeinternational.org/resource/article/examining-twelve-biblical-pillars-male-hierarchy.

5. Lucy Peppiatt, *Rediscovering Scripture's Vision for Women: Fresh Perspectives on Disputed Texts* (Downers Grove, IL: InterVarsity, 2019), 54–55.

6. Laura M. Padilla-Walker, Ashley M. Fraser, and James M. Harper, "Walking the Walk: The Moderating Role of Proactive Parenting on Adolescents' Value-Congruent Behaviors," *Journal of Adolescence* 35, no. 5 (October 2012): 1141–52, https://doi.org/10.1016/j.adolescence.2012.03.003.

7. Emily Wax-Thibodeaux, "'Think of Your Sons': What Parents Can Do in the #MeToo Era," *Washington Post*, October 5, 2018, https://www.washingtonpost.com/nation/2018/10/05/think-your-sons-what-parents-can-do-about-sexual-assault-metoo-era.

8. Elizabeth M. Allard Chamberlain, "Power Play: Sexual Harassment in the Middle School" (PhD diss., University of New Hampshire, Durham, 1997), https://scholars.unh.edu/dissertation/1968.

9. Catherine Hill and Holly Kearl, *Crossing the Line: Sexual Harassment at School* (Washington, DC: American Association of University Women, 2011), 11.

10. Melinda Wenner Moyer, "To Stop Sexual Violence, We Need to Change How We Engage with Kids," *Washington Post*, September 17, 2019, https://www.washingtonpost.com/outlook/2019/09/17/stop-sexual-violence-we-need-change-how-we-engage-with-kids.

11. David McGlynn, "In the #MeToo Era, Raising Boys to Be Good Guys," *New York Times*, June 1, 2018, https://www.nytimes.com/2018/06/01/well/family/metoo-sons-sexual-harassment-parenting-boys.html.

12. Dennis E. Reidy, Joanne P. Smith-Darden, Kai S. Cortina, Roger M. Kernsmith, and Poco D. Kernsmith, "Masculine Discrepancy Stress, Teen Dating Violence, and Sexual Violence Perpetration among Adolescent Boys," *Journal of Adolescent Health* 56, no. 6 (2015): 619–24, https://doi.org/10.1016/j.jadohealth.2015.02.009.

13. "About Fred Rogers," Mister Roger's Neighborhood, https://www.misterrogers.org/about-fred-rogers.

14. Renata Bongiorno, Chloe Langbroek, Paul G. Bain, Michelle Ting, and Michelle K. Ryan, "Why Women Are Blamed for Being Sexually Harassed: The Effects of Empathy for Female Victims and Male Perpetrators," *Psychology of Women Quarterly* 44, no. 1 (March 2020): 11–27, https://doi.org/10.1177/0361684319868730.

15. Wax-Thibodeaux, "'Think of Your Sons.'"

16. "Donald Trump and Jeffrey Epstein Rape Lawsuit Affidavits," filed June 20, 2016, https://www.scribd.com/doc/316341058/Donald-Trump-Jeffrey-Epstein-Rape-Lawsuit-and-Affidavits.

17. David A. Farhenthold, "Trump Recorded Having Extremely Lewd Conversation about Women in 2005," *Washington Post*, October 8, 2016, https://www.washingtonpost.com/politics/trump-recorded-having-extremely-lewd-conversation-about-women-in-2005/2016/10/07/3b9ce776-8cb4-11e6-bf8a-3d26847eeed4_story.html.

18. Sarah Pulliam Bailey, "'Still the Best Candidate': Some Evangelicals Still Back Trump Despite Lewd Video," *Washington Post*, October 8, 2016, https://www.washingtonpost.com/news/acts-of-faith/wp/2016/10/08/still-the-best-candidate-some-evangelicals-still-back-trump-despite-lewd-video.

19. Claire Andre and Manuel Velasquez, "The Just World Theory," Markkula Center for Applied Ethics at Santa Clara University, November 13, 2015, https://www.scu.edu/ethics/ethics-resources/ethical-decision-making/the-just-world-theory.

20. "Why Victims of Sexual Violence Often Stay in Contact with Abusers and Other Key Facts about Trauma," Time's Up, January 4, 2020, https://

timesupfoundation.org/newsroom/weinstein-trial-why-victims-stay-in-touch
-with-perpetrators-and-other-facts.

21. Michael Barbaro and Megan Twohey, "The Woman Defending Harvey
Weinstein," February 7, 2020, in *The Daily*, podcast, https://www.nytimes.com
/2020/02/07/podcasts/the-daily/weinstein-trial.html.

22. Russell L. Meek, "The Burden of Safety Doesn't Lie with the Abused,"
Sojourners, February 13, 2020, https://sojo.net/articles/burden-safety-doesnt
-lie-abused.

Chapter Eleven: He Is Not Indispensable

1. Jericka Duncan, "Pastor Admits to 'Sexual Incident' with Teen 20 Years
Ago, Gets Standing Ovation," *CBS News*, January 9, 2018, https://www.cbs
news.com/news/pastor-admits-to-sexual-incident-with-teen-20-years-ago-gets
-standing-ovation.

2. "Silent No More: A Survivor of Sexual Assault by Prominent Memphis
Pastor Andy Savage Shares Her Story," Watchkeep, January 5, 2018, http://
watchkeep.blogspot.com/2018/01/silent-no-more-survivor-of-sexual.html.

3. Jules Woodson, "I Was Assaulted. He Was Applauded," *New York Times*,
March 9, 2018, https://www.nytimes.com/video/opinion/100000005724879
/i-was-assaulted-he-was-applauded.html.

4. Ed Stetzer, "Andy Savage's Standing Ovation Was Heard Round the
World. Because It Was Wrong," *Christianity Today*, January 11, 2018, https://
www.christianitytoday.com/edstetzer/2018/january/andy-savages-standing
-ovation-was-heard-round-world-because.html.

5. Dave Detling, "Highpoint Church Teaching Pastor Andy Savage An-
nounces Resignation," March 21, 2018, https://www.localmemphis.com
/article/news/local/highpoint-church-teaching-pastor-andy-savage-announ
ces-resignation/522-4670eacc-c0c2-4308-a9a4-7f8c4221c69f.

6. "Force Andy Savage to Resign from Highpoint Church," Change.org,
https://www.change.org/p/megachurch-pastor-receives-standing-ovation
-after-admitting-to-sexual-assault-resign.

7. "TN—Sex Abuse Victims/Advocates Want Church to Act," SNAP, January 28, 2018, https://www.snapnetwork.org/tn_sex_abuse_victims_advocates
_want_church_to_act.

8. "Highpoint's Chris Conlee Gave His Farewell Address as Trustees Apolo-
gizes for Past Mistakes," *Relevant Magazine*, July 18, 2018, https://relevant
magazine.com/current/highpoints-pastor-chris-conlee-has-emotional-fare
well-after-resignation.

9. Michael Gryboski, "Pastor Tied to Andy Savage Sexual Assault Case
Resigns from Texas Church Post," *Christian Post*, February 19, 2018, https://
www.christianpost.com/news/pastor-tied-to-andy-savage-sexual-assault-case
-resigns-from-texas-church-post.html.

10. Victor Xu, "The Full Letter Read by Brock Turner's Father at His
Sentencing Hearing," *Stanford Daily*, June 8, 2016, https://www.stanforddaily
.com/2016/06/08/the-full-letter-read-by-brock-turners-father-at-his-sentenc
ing-hearing.

11. Marina Koren, "Why the Stanford Judge Gave Brock Turner Six Months," *The Atlantic*, June 17, 2016, https://www.theatlantic.com/news/archive/2016/06/stanford-rape-case-judge/487415.

12. Liam Stack, "Light Sentence for Brock Turner in Stanford Rape Case Draws Outrage," *New York Times*, June 6, 2016, https://www.nytimes.com/2016/06/07/us/outrage-in-stanford-rape-case-over-dueling-statements-of-victim-and-attackers-father.html.

13. Daisuke Wakabayashi and Katie Benner, "How Google Protected Andy Rubin, the 'Father of Android,'" *New York Times*, October 25, 2018, https://www.nytimes.com/2018/10/25/technology/google-sexual-harassment-andy-rubin.html.

14. Wakabayashi and Benner, "How Google Protected Andy Rubin."

15. Maggie Astor, "California Voters Remove Judge Aaron Persky, Who Gave a 6-Month Sentence for Sexual Assault," *New York Times*, June 6, 2018, https://www.nytimes.com/2018/06/06/us/politics/judge-persky-brock-turner-recall.html.

16. Jasmine Aguilera, "House Members Unite to Read Stanford Rape Victim's Letter," *New York Times*, June 16, 2016, https://www.nytimes.com/2016/06/17/us/politics/congress-stanford-letter.html.

17. Daisuke Wakabayashi, Erin Griffith, Amie Tsang, and Kate Conger, "Google Walkout: Employees Stage Protest over Handling of Sexual Harassment," *New York Times*, November, 1, 2018, https://www.nytimes.com/2018/11/01/technology/google-walkout-sexual-harassment.html.

18. Wakabayashi et al., "Google Walkout."

Chapter Twelve: Believe Women

1. Josephus, *Antiquities of the Jews* 4.219, in Flavius Josephus, *The Works of Flavius Josephus*, translated by William Whiston (A.M. Auburn and Buffalo, NY: John E. Beardsley, 1895), 119.

2. Jessica Valenti and Jaclyn Friedman, *Believe Me: How Trusting Women Can Change the World* (New York: Seal, 2020), 2–3.

3. Mischa Haider, "The Next Step in #MeToo Is for Men to Reckon with Their Male Fragility," *Slate*, January 23, 2019, https://slate.com/news-and-politics/2019/01/men-male-fragility-metoo-progress.html.

4. Shayna Jacobs, "Harvey Weinstein Sentenced to 23 Years in Prison for Sexually Assaulting Two Women in New York," *Washington Post*, March 11, 2020, https://www.washingtonpost.com/lifestyle/harvey-weinstein-sentence-trial-sexual-assault/2020/03/11/398f2cf6-630b-11ea-acca-80c22bbee96f_story.html.

5. Lia Beck, "Where R. Kelly's Legal Cases Stand in 2020," *Refinery 29*, January 3, 2020, https://www.refinery29.com/en-us/2020/01/9133830/where-is-r-kelly-today-legal-cases-updates.

6. Whitney Friedlander, "Lifetime Plans Follow-Up to 'Surviving R. Kelly' and Jeffrey Epstein Documentary," CNN, July 24, 2019, https://www.cnn.com/2019/07/23/entertainment/surviving-r-kelly-surviving-jeffrey-epstein/index.html.

7. Robert Downen, Lise Olsen, and John Tedesco, "Abuse of Faith," *Houston Chronicle*, February 10, 2019, https://www.houstonchronicle.com/news/investigations/article/Southern-Baptist-sexual-abuse-spreads-as-leaders-13588038.php.

8. Holly Meyer, "Texas Church Expelled from Southern Baptist Convention for Hiring Registered Sex Offender as Pastor," *Tennessean*, February 18, 2020, https://www.tennessean.com/story/news/religion/2020/02/18/texas-church-expelled-southern-baptist-convention-hiring-registered-sex-offender-pastor/4788165002.

9. Leo Shane III, "Defense Department to Make Sexual Harassment a Crime, *Military Times*, May 2, 2019, https://www.militarytimes.com/news/pentagon-congress/2019/05/02/defense-department-to-make-sexual-harassment-a-crime.

10. Amanda Rossie Barroso, "The Myth of a #MeToo Generational Divide," National Women's Law Center, November 13, 2018, https://nwlc.org/blog/the-myth-of-a-metoo-generational-divide.

11. Jane van Dis, Laura Stadum, and Esther Choo, "Sexual Harassment Is Rampant in Healthcare. Here's How to Stop It," *Harvard Business Review*, November 1, 2018, https://hbr.org/2018/11/sexual-harassment-is-rampant-in-health-care-heres-how-to-stop-it.

12. Norbert Juma, "60 Ruth Bader Ginsburg Quotes on Standing for Justice," Everyday Power, September 24, 2020, https://everydaypower.com/ruth-bader-ginsburg-quotes.

13. Clare Foran, "How to Design a City for Women," *CityLab*, September 16, 2013, https://www.citylab.com/transportation/2013/09/how-design-cit-women/6739.

14. Jie Chen, Woon Sau Leung, Wei Song, and Marc Goergen, "Research: When Women Are on Boards, Male CEOs Are Less Overconfident," *Harvard Business Review*, September 12, 2019, https://hbr.org/2019/09/research-when-women-are-on-boards-male-ceos-are-less-overconfident.

15. "Facts and Figures: Economic Empowerment," UN Women, last updated July 2018, https://www.unwomen.org/en/what-we-do/economic-empowerment/facts-and-figures.

16. Jonathan Woetzel, Anu Madgavkar, Kweilin Ellingrud, Eric Labaye, Sandrine Devillard, Eric Kutcher, James Manyika, Richard Dobbs, and Mekala Krishnan, "How Advancing Women's Equality Can Add $12 Trillion to Global Growth," McKinsey Global Institute, September 1, 2015, https://www.mckinsey.com/featured-insights/employment-and-growth/how-advancing-womens-equality-can-add-12-trillion-to-global-growth.

17. Michael S. Rosenwald, "No Women Served on the Senate Judiciary Committee in 1991. The Ugly Anita Hill Hearings Changed That," *Washington Post*, September 18, 2018, https://www.washingtonpost.com/history/2018/09/18/no-women-served-senate-judiciary-committee-ugly-anita-hill-hearings-changed-that.

18. Elaine Godfrey and Russell Berman, "The Real Turning Point for Women's Political Power," *The Atlantic*, July 2, 2019, https://www.theatlantic

.com/politics/archive/2019/07/how-women-remade-american-government-after-suffrage/591940.

19. Beyoncé, "Run the World (Girls)," Genius, https://genius.com/Beyonce-run-the-world-girls-lyrics.

20. "Open Letter Concerning Rev. Donald 'Bud' Heckman," United Methodist Young Clergywomen Collective, February 10, 2020, http://umyoungclergywomen.com/2020/02/10/open-letter-concerning-rev-donald-bud-heckman/#more-117.

21. Emily McFarlan Miller, "United Methodist #MeToo Complaint against Bud Heckman Settled," *Religion News Service,* January 3, 2020, https://religionnews.com/2020/01/03/united-methodist-metoo-complaint-ends-in-resolution-between-clergyman-denomination.

22. Heather Hahn, "#MeToo Case Ends with Surrendered Credentials," *UM News,* June 11, 2020, https://www.umnews.org/en/news/me-too-case-ends-with-surrendered-credentials.

Tiffany Bluhm is the author of *She Dreams* and *Never Alone* and their companion Bible studies. She is a speaker, writer, and podcast cohost of *Why Tho*, a show answering the existential and nonsensical questions we ask ourselves. She speaks at conferences and events around the world. Her work has been featured in *World Vision* magazine and *Pentecostal Evangel*, and on the YouVersion Bible app, the Hallmark Channel, the *Jenny McCarthy Show*, and more. She leads an engaged audience of fifty thousand followers online and is committed to encouraging people of faith to live lives of conviction, substance, and grace. As a minority immigrant woman with an interracial family, Bluhm is passionate about inviting all to the table of faith, equality, justice, and dignity.